FARMER SUTRA

The true story of how a city dweller realised her farm dream

KALPANA MANIVANNAN

An imprint of
Srishti Publishers & Distributors

Srishti Publishers & Distributors
A unit of AJR Publishing LLP
212A, Peacock Lane, Shahpur Jat,
New Delhi - 110 049

editorial@srishtipublishers.com

First published by Bold,
an imprint of Srishti Publishers & Distributors in 2023

10 9 8 7 6 5 4 3 2 1

This is a work of non-fiction, based on the author's thorough research and experience. Some events have been fictionalised for dramatic effect. While due care has been taken to verify all information at press time, any inadvertent miss brought to notice shall be updated in the subsequent editions.

Printed and bound in India

Dedicated to the
Organic Farming communities,
to the Earthkeepers,

And to Mani –
for believing in my audacious dream.

Prologue

December 2019

"Want some tea?" My voice came out in a whisper. We had been in the garden all day and had just about managed to drag our tired bodies to a shady spot under the banana grove. My husband finally nodded in the affirmative, as we leaned on each other for support. Our garden stretched out in our line of vision as I pondered; not over the work done, but how far we had come.

"How did I reach here? Where did I gather the courage to overcome the 'what ifs'? How did I manage to reach the farthest edges of my farm dream and how in the world did we create what I had only seen in my mind's eye? Is this for real? How did we...?" I mumbled.

Mani turned to look at me and smiled, and I knew that I didn't have to finish the thought. Such moments had become more frequent now and something told me that we would relive and savour them many times over. We sipped our tea in silence as the sun got ready to set on the horizon, painting the sky in myriad shades of orange, pink and yellow.

***

A forgotten memory of creating a flower garden suddenly made its appearance as I took a break from making big compost pits around my fruit trees. Piling compost, dried leaves, cow dung manure and wood ash layer by layer into huge pits was an exhausting task, but an exhilarating one as well. The pomegranate, mango, guava, sapota, sweet lime and jamun tree saplings had been looking miserable and neglected, left to their own devices, as we had been pouring our attention on our vegetable patches lately. I looked on, happy in the knowledge that today, my trees had been shown some love and undivided attention, besides the heaps of nourishment.

At a distance, under the banana trees, my farm-helpers were taking a break. I could see Vasanthi talking animatedly to Rani while she pulled out her stainless steel lunch box from her wire basket as they settled down to have their lunch. Saroja was laughing as she walked towards the other two. Their chatter and squeals could be heard over the water gushing out from a bore well in the neighbouring farm.

As I sat on one of the benches under the coconut trees, the breeze felt heavenly and delicious against my sun-ravaged body. We had come to call this space the 'four-tree point' because, well, there were four palm trees growing almost equidistant from each other, forming a closed canopy that hardly allowed a few rays of sunlight to pierce through their fronds. We had built four brick benches outlining the periphery of the square formed between those trees, making it the perfect spot for our breaks.

The air was filled with chirps, coos and cock-a-doodles and I was drawn to the birdsongs. There was a cacophony of sounds; melodious whistles overlapping with steady cooing interspersed with some loud cawing as I tried to identify the birds by those sounds. The serenity under these trees wrapped me in an instant calming embrace.

I took a moment to admire all the work we had completed since we arrived early that day. There was still so much more to be done post lunch before I could mentally tick off the to-do list. But for now, my eyes seemed to momentarily stop at the farmhouse entrance. That forgotten memory of wanting to create a picturesque and inviting front yard came back to me.

The randomly planted flowering shrubs hadn't turned out the way I envisioned. The few that had adapted well had ended up looking like an overgrown shrubbery while the less-fortunate ones had withered away, leaving behind large unsightly gaps. The colour scheme looked completely off too. I remembered going for a layered look of white and blue flowers with a mix of milder tones of peaches and greens here and there, but what I saw was nothing close to that. The space had been completely hijacked by the red fountain plant, purple angelonia and white crepe jasmines. I paused. Okay, so what exactly was I expecting to see?

Creating a layered garden required years of landscaping experience and here I was chiding myself for not being able to recreate a replica of a garden seen in glossy gardening magazines at my very first attempt!

That memory of creating a bustling patch of colourful blooms in front of our farmhouse had been carelessly tossed aside and left by the window some years ago, when my whole being was consumed with building a food forest.

Now, with a thriving food forest in place, it was time to pick up the daydream from that forgotten spot and weave it into the fabric of reality. This little dream, like all the others, hit me with a sense of urgency. They had never been patient with me. There was an instant flurry, a new surge of energy that pierced through, creating a mild disturbance in my peaceful existence. I felt this turbulence every time I was about to achieve a state of peace that came with achieving a dream of mine. Just when I thought I could finally sit back and relax, there came another one swooping down on me vying for my attention. Before I knew it, I was already sucked into it and engulfed by the sheer excitement of making it come alive.

I was now all pumped up about the flower garden dream, but I knew it had to wait for just a little while longer. I'd need to put on my learner's hat for this one and dive deep into growing flowers and landscaping before I could get anything done close to the picture I had in my mind. Until then, I'd have to make do with living vicariously through other people's beautiful garden pictures.

After a whole day of weeding and manuring, our bodies had given in as we broke for lunch. The hot April air felt heavy as I walked leisurely towards our farmhouse where I had kept the lunch bag. I found Mani washing banana leaves over the kitchen sink. We ate our lunch on banana leaves whenever we were at the farm because that was a luxury we couldn't afford in the city. Over lunch, we discussed our plans for the rest of the day before it was time to head back to the city.

I spotted the ladies settled under the shade of trees to rest. As we stretched out our tired limbs, I wondered if we could grab a quick snooze as well. Through the open door, I saw the new watermelon seedlings bobbing their heads gently in the breeze. This year looked like a success for the watermelon patch. We had tried twice earlier, but the seedlings hadn't survived. The timing seemed right and the seeds did germinate, but I guess the soil was the culprit. I realised that we hadn't taken enough care to build the soil before planting the watermelons earlier. Except for the raised beds where we prepared the soil well for planting, the other areas on the farm weren't suitable for crops due to the predominant clayey structure of the soil.

So, this time around, I took my time to build the soil well before planting the watermelon seeds. From the looks of it, it seemed like we might finally get to taste them this summer after all. My eyelids got heavy and the watermelon patch slowly blurred and dissolved from my range of vision.

A loud chuckle followed by sounds of women giggling startled me, jolting me out of my short but sweet siesta. It seemed like I had been dreaming but I couldn't quite remember what it was about. I felt a bit disoriented as I had never taken a nap during a farm day before and it took a while for my eyes to adjust to the surroundings. The workers were back at their jobs with their loud banter and just like that, we were back to work.

Chapter 1

2013

"You know, we must clear up that piece of land on Raja Street and start a vegetable garden there. The land is simply going to waste. It doesn't look like we have any plans of building a house there anytime soon, so why not put it to good use? Just imagine how lovely it would be to drive up on weekends and come back with a loaded car with the week's harvest." That was me talking to Mani in a trance-like state as my mind was picturing a garden bursting with colourful veggies with me harvesting a basketful of the bounty.

For the umpteenth time, my husband heard me out first and said, "That piece of land is an overgrown jungle of weeds now and the last time I checked, it's officially the neighbourhood's dump yard. How do you propose we plan on clearing all that debris, preparing the land, procuring water supply and growing the plants of your dreams? Have you considered the time, money and the labour it asks for? How do you plan on taking care of the plants on a daily basis?"

Oh, did I mention, we lived almost one and a half hours away from *that* plot and that both of us were gainfully employed with two school-going kids to manage between us.

With that reality check, I was jolted out of my sweet reverie into the real world with its real issues. This was probably the zillionth fantasising session for me. Mani, on the other hand, didn't possess a single daydreaming bone in him and was way too practical to indulge in my dream fest, not even for a fleeting moment. Now, was it necessary for him to bring me to the real world with a thud? Well, what could I say? He was the sane, down to earth person with his head firmly placed on his shoulders; unlike me, the eternal dreamer.

I am glad he was the way he was and I was the way I was because I had realised in all these years of being married to each other that we needed both these characteristic traits in equal measure for a good balance; though I secretly felt that Mani put up with my nonsensical talk because somewhere deep down he too liked the idea, but was too practical to know that there was no room for that kind of a lifestyle in our existing scheme of things.

Though I was back into the real world and acting all grown-up and responsible, this period of clarity usually didn't last long until the same insanity resurfaced in me in a few weeks' time or, if my husband was lucky enough, maybe in a few months. And the same conversation would follow with minor variations here and there.

Coming from a middle-class South Indian background, we were fed on a steady diet of hard work and duty consciousness. The primary focus of our education and upbringing was to work hard, take care of the family and the siblings and ensure everyone had settled down well. Once that was taken care of, we had to start saving enough to afford the standard Indian middle-class dream – a 2 BHK apartment in the city, a decent car, two (well-behaved) kids, an annual vacation and a retirement fund.

We had been working hard towards the fulfilment of 'the Dream'. Mani's IT profession had taken us to the US where we spent a few good years chasing the quintessential dream. After our return to India four years ago, we sought our kids' school admissions, rented an apartment in a convenient locality and applied for a set of loans for a car and a place of our own.

My days were occupied with settling into a routine: getting the lunches packed, getting the kids bathed, fed and out of the house in time for school and managing a job I had taken up as a teacher. All four of us ran a race against time on most working days. We were grateful for weekends so we could rest our weary bones, stock up on the grocery supplies for the forthcoming week, play catch up with the piling laundry and spend time as a family. We had perfected this rigmarole and things went on like clockwork as the years passed by.

Just before returning to India, we had decided to invest in a small piece of land in a good residential neighbourhood where we could build our dream house. No sooner had we settled in India, it became evident that living in an independent house might not be such a good idea. Safety was the biggest concern for residents of metro cities and Chennai wasn't any different. Besides, with our kids aged six and two and a half years, it dawned on us that their social interactions would be hindered if we lived in an independent house.

Living in an apartment complex gave us this much needed perspective. With a round-the-clock security system and the comfort of kids playing with their friends within safe confines, community living offered something an independent house could not have provided us. With that newfound perspective, the idea of building a house on that piece of property was temporarily shelved. Though we had taken a huge loan to purchase that land, much to our chagrin, it continued to remain unused.

As we settled in and things started falling into a predictable routine, I started to dream about using that piece of land effectively. Every once in a while, I'd voice those audacious dreams and even bravely discuss the possibility of growing our own vegetables, of setting-up farm stands, of farmers' markets and Sunday farm visits. All this fantasising happened while sipping coffee on the little balcony of our rented apartment on weekend mornings. It was just one of those dreams you have – nice to talk about, but didn't really have any potential of materialising.

Years rolled by as life took precedence with our jobs, kids, school and extra-curricular activities, planning meals, meeting family and friends, birthdays and so on. With time, we moved into another rented apartment closer to school and work. It was as if days were flying and I suddenly found my pre-schooler and kindergartener in primary and middle school.

Where did the time go? I liked to think of myself as someone who was mindful and intentional about making the most of the time with her kids, but I could feel time slipping out of my hands. Mani said time flew when you were having a good time, yet I couldn't help but feel the ache of my kids outgrowing my lap so soon.

***

It was 2014 and we had finally moved into our own apartment and slid comfortably into our lifestyle yet again. With our workplace a stone's throw away from our house, things couldn't be better. Life had taken a predictable rhythm and with the kids a little older – one being 9 and the other, 13 – things were much smoother. The grocery shopping and supermarket visits made up for weekend family time with an occasional mall visit thrown in for good measure.

Ever since we moved back from the US, I could sense a visible shift in the city's infrastructure. The steadily increasing malls and supermarkets were strategically wiping away the little corner shops, the small grocers and barber shops. In just a few years, the whole landscape of the city had changed tremendously. When we had first moved to this end of the city, it was a sleepy little town with its paddy fields on one side and little houses on the other, still untouched by the glittery cityscape. We would shop at little corner shops for weekly groceries and for kids' stationery needs and would trudge all the way to the more happening part of the city only occasionally for bigger purchases.

Slowly with years, buildings and apartment complexes started mushrooming around. Online shopping and door-to-door delivery ushered in a consumerist lifestyle that was addictive and kept us away from venturing into any uncomfortable zone of going down the path less travelled. We were hooked to this convenience-driven life and followed the pied pipers (read giant corporations) as they led the way.

While this was very convenient for our busy lifestyle, I started noticing a growing uneasiness in me. The quality of food and commodities that we procured for our family started plaguing me. I was reading more and more about the menace of chemically grown produce and the alarming rates of food adulterations. It was unnerving for me to read studies showing food industries flouting safety regulations and going beyond permissible limits, making it hazardous for our health.

This realisation drove me into a frantic search for organic sources within the city limits, but it was proving to be a challenge with many dubious labels claiming to be organic to fool gullible consumers. My inability to do anything about it was frustrating me. In the midst of all this, the dream of growing my own vegetables kept resurfacing now and then, only to get squashed with a heavy dose of reality.

With every passing year, our job responsibilities kept steadily increasing too, but things were about to change, and I didn't have an inkling whatsoever that my dream was about to get its wings.

Chapter 2

January 2016

Mani groggily walked towards the front door to pick up the day's newspaper and I headed to the kitchen to brew some coffee as the Sunday morning stretched lazily.

I rolled up the bamboo blinds and almost instantly, the sunrays hit my eyes, making me squint. I adjusted my eyes and lifted my face to the sun to feel its warmth. As I stretched myself, I relished the morning light flooding the kitchen.

The east-facing window was a blessing; I got to see the sun rising on the horizon every day. On a clear day, if I really focused, I could see the coastline at the farthest range of my vision, even with all the skyscrapers and concrete jungle coming in the way.

I placed a kettle of water to boil, scooped out three heaped teaspoons full of coffee powder and dropped it into the stainless steel filter. The aroma was intoxicating and filled up my nostrils. I heard the water come up to a roaring boil and poured it into the filter for the decoction to trickle down. It would easily take ten minutes for it to be ready, so I walked into the living room.

I found Mani comfortably sitting crisscross on the floor with the newspaper spread wide open in front of him. Though we had a large, comfortable L-shaped seven-seater sofa and a dining set, we still preferred sitting on the floor in the space between the furniture most of the time. He was bent over it, pouring through the headlines. Except for the occasional flipping of the newspaper, there was not a sound. The kids were fast asleep and there was a certain Zen-like peace prevailing around me. As I sat beside him, he pulled out the supplementary edition and handed it to me almost instinctively, even while being deeply engrossed in reading. I took it and started browsing mindlessly, wondering how this scene played out exactly, with clockwork precision, on most Sundays.

We had definitely become creatures of habit. I was reminded of my parents and their habitual ways of doing things. I suddenly felt old thinking of how couples married for long years become accustomed to certain set ways of doing things. Instead of feeling miffed at this sudden realisation of the age factor, I was actually feeling all warm and fuzzy. With age, we had arrived at a point in life where we finally felt settled and less flustered, unlike when we were younger.

A gentle breeze riffled the newspaper, disturbing the stillness a bit. As Mani struggled to hold it in place, I looked up towards the direction of the breeze. I saw my ivory-coloured sheer curtains flipping gently over the French doors that slide open into the balcony. My eyes came to rest at the striking image of the bright pink and white bougainvillea dancing in the breeze, out in the balcony. They trailed beautifully on the railings, covering a portion of the grill. I recalled wanting to plant them when I started setting up the balcony garden. This was exactly what I wanted to look at every morning from my living room.

I found myself reminiscing about how much I had immersed in designing this space for us. Every little detail, from the wall paint to a miniscule artefact, was given a lot of thought and time. Months of researching, picking and choosing had gone into making this a perfect haven for us. For years we had been shifting from one rented place to another and when we finally got to settle down in our very own house, I might have gone overboard. I wanted this space to be warm and sophisticated at the same time, and since Mani had absolutely no interest in the design aspect, the reins were in my hands.

After a lot of contemplation on colour scheme, I kept gravitating towards the idea of a white, earthy look for the living room; I always found that to be elegant. So, the living area mostly has tones of brown and beige with pearl-white walls. I couldn't believe the insane amount of time and effort I took to pick the curtains, but it was so worth it. The chocolate brown floor to ceiling curtains with intricate gold and muted blue detailing were simply luxurious. They perfectly complemented the whites and neutrals in the space. When it came to the accent walls, I remembered stressing over whether to go for wood-panelling or wallpaper. I saw the champagne gold-coloured wallpaper with its subtle pattern and metallic undertones, beautifully blending in with the cedar brown decorative cabinets mounted over it and I thought I had made the right choice.

I was suddenly overcome with such an intense joy that I don't think my heart could hold it in. This was a culmination of years of yearning I had carried within me; to create that perfect look for the house I could call my own someday. I was usually never this appreciative of any of my work; my brain is trained to instantly look for all the things that went wrong and how certain aspects didn't turn out as I had intended, but not that day. I was surprised to be pleased and satisfied with all the things that were once just a figment of my imagination.

I noticed it was about time and my coffee decoction must be ready. I got up, grinning from ear to ear, totally overcome with gratitude. By the time I brought in two steaming mugs of coffee, Mani was reading the sports section, his favourite part of the newspaper. I sometimes wondered if he got the newspaper just to read the sports news!

This was pretty much our regular Sunday that completely ran on auto-pilot, except for the nostalgic little detour that I took that day. The day was progressing as usual until Mani, for no particular reason, started browsing through the classifieds and something seemed to catch his fancy.

"A ten-ground property with coconut palms for sale," he read out loud. I looked at him in confusion as I sipped my coffee. I assumed he was just making idle conversation, pulling my leg with the farmland hope as he went back to reading. Dismissing it as a casual remark, I turned my attention to my perfect cup; extra strong, just the way I liked it.

"What do you think about this? Wouldn't it be cool to have a small coconut farm?" Mani remarked absentmindedly, a minute later.

I looked at him, bewildered. He sure seemed quite taken with this, but I refused to be sucked into it, knowing well that it would rekindle the old dream of mine that I had finally managed to bury in the dark confines of my subconscious mind. Just when I had relinquished that thought, he'd better not spring this on me. Oh no, I was not falling for it!

"You never showed any inclination towards buying a farm before. What's gotten into you?" I asked nonchalantly. This was so unlike him; to do anything on a whim, leave alone buying a piece of land. Despite my better judgement, my mind had already taken off into weaving a little image of the farm. I was secretly enjoying it but I didn't show it. What if he really *was* just teasing me? I was someone who got carried away very soon and then once I started dreaming, I didn't want it to come crashing down, so I tried to be cautious and not fall for it.

"Just imagine; a coconut farm less than an hour away!" Mani was gleefully looking at the advertisement.

Okay! That was enough. I was about to lose it.

"Are you kidding me? Don't even joke about it, you hear me?" I said, mocking a threatening tone. "Do you think we can even afford this right now?" I let that slide slowly.

"Let's check it out and then decide."

With that, he picked up his phone and proceeded to call the number given in the advertisement. I stared at him in disbelief, forgetting that my coffee was going cold. This was getting a little too serious. I was oddly excited and nervous at the same time. I left my coffee aside and watched him intently.

There was a sudden rush of energy and exhilaration. My mind was on overdrive and there was a strange electric sensation coursing through my body. There was a buzz in the air and the energy in the room abruptly transformed into something thrilling. From having a mundane morning, we were now contemplating buying a small farmland! Could we really? Was it possible?

After the initial enquiry, he sounded pleased by whatever the person on the other side was telling him.

"Sure, absolutely. We can come right away!" I heard conviction in Mani's parting words. We were still in our nightclothes and the kids were deep in sleep. There was no way we could "come right away" at any rate.

"Get ready, we are leaving in five minutes," he said, putting the phone away and scrabbling through the narrow hallway towards the master bedroom. I was stunned. All through this, I had been sitting like a zombie, unable to move and wondering if this was really happening, or was I imagining all of it?

"Hurry up!" Mani called out from the room.

What happened after that is still a blur because we were ready in a jiffy to drive down to wherever this place was. The kids were still blissfully sleeping and we just quietly woke my elder one to inform her that we would be back in about two hours or so. She murmured something in the line of acknowledgement and I gave the basic instructions of not opening the door for anyone and to keep an eye on her brother and that we would be back before they were up.

Just like that, we were in the car following the directions over the phone. There was a nervous, tingling sensation in my body as all this felt surreal. We drove past the city that was just waking up lazily on a Sunday morning. Except for the few joggers and an occasional tea shop that was open, the roads looked deserted. We continued for about half an hour and reached the quaint outskirts.

Naveen, the seller, was waiting for us at the suggested place and waved at us with a broad welcoming smile. He walked over to our car and introduced himself. We followed his car that took a turn into a mud road, and the scenario around changed abruptly. We were suddenly transported to a hinterland with long stretches of paddy fields, grazing cows, villagers huddled around chatting and herds of goats that made us slam the brakes frequently.

We followed Naveen and saw him pulling over into a huge open space in the middle of nowhere. When we got down and walked around, we noticed the backwaters at a distance. Except for that, there wasn't anything else around in sight. Naveen took us around and showed us the length and breadth of the property. Mani and I exchanged a quick glance and we both knew instantly that it wasn't exactly what we had in mind.

This was turning out to be a total waste of my precious time on the rare Sundays I got to rest. I ruefully chided myself and wondered when does it ever happen that a dream property was bought over on the very first visit? Or any property for that matter. I knew because we have changed houses many times over in the last fifteen years of our married life.

I heard Mani politely say, "Naveen, this is a great place, but you see, we were expecting to see a coconut farm nestled someplace a little more, umm... secure." As nothing fruitful was going to happen, in a bid to save the rest of the Sunday, I signalled Mani to end the pleasantries and get going.

As soon as we finished our sentence, Naveen jumped in, saying, "Sir, I have just the place you are looking for. I was about to show you that next, but before that, I thought you might want to check this one out. That's why I brought you here."

"Ah, is it?" Mani shot a glance at me over his shoulder. This time around, I was a little more practical than usual and told myself that this was just another one of those salesman gimmicks. I decided to drop all my expectations to zero because I hated getting my hopes high only to end up utterly disappointed.

I mentally resigned myself to the fact that the trip was a waste of time and turned around to see Naveen weaving his charm on Mani with his words and easy cheerful banter, just like a typical salesman, but also somehow coming off as a genuine guy. I already saw that he had convinced Mani into seeing this other property which seemed to be just down the road and so, we decided to check it out.

The road leading up to the property slowly turned into a weathered dirt road and right at the bend was a small temple. Just across from it was a big temple tank that was filled with pink lotus blooms and white water lilies. It had steps built on all four sides and wore a slightly dilapidated look with moss covering the lower steps, but didn't look too bad either. There were large trees on the banks of it, entwined with other smaller trees and creepers growing nearby. The periphery of the tank lined with palm trees all around made for a picturesque view.

"Why are you smiling?" Mani threw me a glance quizzically as he manoeuvred the car to turn left. In absorbing all of the beautiful scenery around me, I didn't realise I was smiling.

"Huh... oh, I like this place. Isn't it beautiful?" I replied dreamily.

"Yeah, it's nice," Mani replied matter-of-factly, looking around as if noticing the surroundings just then. He turned his attention back to following Naveen, who was leading the way.

As the car rolled down the mud road, everything around me seemed to slow down. The coconut palms were gently swaying in the breeze, the paddy fields lush and in all hues of green abound as far as my eyes could see. I saw small hutments dotting the fields and motor pumps with water gushing out. As we took a right turn, I saw Naveen's car pulling up on the side.

My eyes started scanning the place as I tried fervently to locate the property; and there it was, tucked away from the main road yet not completely secluded. There were around thirty fully grown coconut trees in the small half-acre property and a beautiful makeshift treehouse built on four old palm trunks on one side.

I noticed Mani beaming and I knew at that moment that we had found our farm; it was love at first sight for us. I realised that we hadn't even openly discussed what we thought of it. I couldn't even recall if we really spoke about it; just the big smile on our faces was proof enough. Words weren't necessary.

In retrospect, I think Naveen didn't have to do any convincing; no sales-pitch was needed whatsoever. We were sold from the moment we laid eyes on the property. He must have realised we were such easy targets; foolish buyers who didn't know how to play the game of property buying – the disinterested looks, pointing out reasons why it wasn't such a great buy, the haggling and bargaining and the usual stuff property buying involved.

You were to never show that you were eager to purchase; you should play the 'hard to please' game. That was how it was supposed to be done, but both Mani and I were terrible actors. We couldn't act to save our lives. We were pleased and it showed, and that was that!

There was a beautiful peepul tree intertwined with two coconut palms right in the middle of the farm, and it looked mesmerising. I had never seen anything like it. The location was just right, with a mix of comfortable privacy and safe public access. To lure us even more, a quick drive around the place revealed that this place was actually in the middle of a quiet little village.

Nearby was a huge banyan tree with about eight to ten prop roots transformed into peripheral stems supporting the huge canopy, resembling a *mandapam*. A small group of villagers were resting under its shade with a few make-shift *thottil* made out of old sarees hanging from the branches, cradling the napping babies under the cool breeze. The serene backwaters, which we had noticed while visiting the earlier property, were just a stone's throw away. That kind of sealed the deal for us.

The wonderful turn of events had shushed my inner critic; my usual dreamy self was back and I had already started visualising wonderful picnics and friends' meet-up there. With a small cottage-style farmhouse, a vegetable garden, a pergola with lots of bougainvillea and some stone-lined winding pathways in the garden, it would be delightful indeed.

A weekend getaway from the hustle and bustle of city life; many quiet afternoons lazing on the hammocks with a book; picnics under fruit trees; barbecue dinners under the stars; now, wouldn't that be lovely!

That was how it all started; just like that...

Chapter 3

March 2016

"Yeah, sure! Of course, we can come by on Thursday." Mani was talking into the phone.

I looked up from the answer scripts I was correcting. Did 'we' involve me? I wondered. He threw a glance at me and continued to talk to the person on the line. I went back to my papers. *Why couldn't students follow a simple instruction on writing important features in bullet points? They had written detailed stories describing something that just needed to be stated in half a sentence. This was a science paper, for god's sake, not creative writing!*

I made a mental note to reiterate these pointers for the zillionth time in all the sections of grade 10. They couldn't be presenting their answers in this manner in their boards. *Oh and this! Not again... if I see one more student misspell menstruation as mensuration, I am going to lose it.* Woes of being a biology teacher. I made a big red circle around the word and wrote a remark on the margin as Mani walked in.

"You'll have to apply for leave on Thursday, K," Mani declared as he hung up the phone.

"I don't think I can. Exams are going on at school. It will be quite challenging to—"

"We need to go to the sub-registrar's office for the land registration that day. It was Naveen on the phone. He has fixed the dates for our registration," Mani interrupted before I could finish.

"Oh... Ohhh... Wow! That's wonderful!" I could hear myself squealing in delight.

"I cannot believe this is happening. I'll talk to Principal ma'am and apply for leave immediately," I told him as I processed the entire scene in my mind. Oh, I'd need to sit with my substitution team tomorrow and work it out.

Of course, I'd have to cross-check the whole exam duty circular with the substitution duty checklist before it went out tomorrow. Chances were I'd probably have to redo the entire thing I had worked on for hours, but it had to be done. Managing the duties of a high school teacher and an academic coordinator was surely getting quite hectic. I made a mental note to get it done first thing the next morning. With that, I got back to my answer scripts. No matter how hard I focused, I was unable to attack the stack of papers with the same fervour as before. After a few failed attempts at bringing my mojo back, I dropped the red pen, rested my head on the sofa, closed my eyes and smiled. Well, there went the target I had set for completion of this bundle! The mister could have held on to the good news a little while longer. But the damage was done.

Ever since we'd seen this little coconut farm on that bright sunny morning, the dream of living there wasn't letting me sleep. I was completely immersed in reading up everything about farming that I could lay my hands on, in whatever little free time I got. I could visualise myself drawn towards the homesteading, aka the 'DIY' lifestyle.

Never in my wildest imagination would I have thought of homesteading till a couple of years back. I don't know what had gotten into me. I kept talking about having a cow at our farm. Yes, a cow! Make it two, actually. I had names picked out for them – Lakshmi and Gowri. For the sake of perspective, while these conversations were happening, we were yet to become the legal farm owners.

The upcoming months went into registering the property and other documentation work. Government offices were amongst those places where you developed patience by virtue of being there. Who needed the mighty Himalayas? This was a much quicker, easier and not to mention cheaper way to achieve nirvana. If you have ever dealt with any government-related work, you know what I mean.

So, the D-day of registration arrived and after sending the kids off to school, we rushed to get ourselves ready for the day. I picked a mildly festive salwar-kameez, a pastel green one with a delicate silver line detail running along the edges of the sleeves and a bit of embroidery on the yoke. Mani looked at me quizzically as he brushed his hair, just a split-second longer than usual, and I knew what he was thinking.

"Well, we *are* registering the property today and it is a big day for us. We are going to be the official owners of a little farm soon. It's a special day for us!"

Mani nodded in mild amusement as he picked up the phone to call Naveen. We got into the car as he updated the plan on meeting up at the sub-registrar's office that was an hour away from our place. I switched on Google Maps and sat back, allowing the foreign lady's voice to guide us in her American accent. As we moved away from the city and towards the narrower by-lanes of a more rural Kanchipuram area, the lady started butchering the street names and it reached the peak of incomprehensibility. We had great fun figuring out her pronunciation. Though it was downright pathetic, I have to agree it was mildly comical too. What was important was that she ensured we reached our destination on time.

It was a small town with narrow lanes forking into even smaller streets lined with many *pettikadai* with a sprinkling of tea stalls and tiffin centres. Interspersed were some ancient, terracotta tiled houses in dilapidated conditions with their characteristic *thinnai*, a seating area in the frontage of the house. It turned out that these houses had been converted into notary public offices and printing shops, probably owing to the registrar's office being on this street. Pedestrians were scampering about on foot, some people on bicycles, with rarely a bike or two whizzing past, painting a distinct old-worldly look to the place.

We carefully circumnavigated the locality to locate a spot to park our car, and amidst curious stares from the onlookers, we finally managed to find a space just a little further along from the office.

Naveen, who was already waiting for us at the gate, accompanied us inside where we were asked to wait. With no waiting area of sorts, people were scattered around the place and hanging out chit-chatting wherever they could find space. Mani found a spot on the steps of the office building and settled down to take his office calls. I looked at the dusty steps and decided to stand and wait.

After half an hour, we impatiently inquired but were told to wait again. Two hours later, there were no signs of any advancement in the situation. I sceptically dusted a spot next to Mani and sat down hesitantly. Lunch time came and went, still nothing.

That was when it dawned on me that we were in a government office and there was going to be a lot of waiting around before we got anything done. We had been given an appointment for 10 a.m.; it was 3 p.m. and still nothing. By now, I was tired, my hair was all dishevelled and my back hurt from sitting all day in a slouchy position on the stairs.

With nothing much to do, I resorted to the only possible thing to pass time. I looked on as people scurried in and out of the building. I saw someone walk past me carrying a flask and some paper cups inside the building. I got a whiff of cardamom tea wafting in the air. Before I could smile at the thought of tea, a sigh escaped me as the tea break for the officials just meant more waiting for us.

My gaze hovered beyond the premises, across the narrow road, and I saw small crowds starting to gather around the tiny tea stalls as the tea master deftly ladled out mugs of tea. The way he lifted the mug up in the air as far up as his arms could reach and then made a sharp descent dramatically, leaving the glass tumbler frothing, was sheer poetry. I had been intrigued by this little dance and found that there was a name to this art form –'pulling the tea'. The froth looked menacingly close to overflowing the edges of the tumbler but stopped right at the edge as if at the command of its master, as he handed it to the eager customer who was clearly taken by this visual treat and welcomed it with a broad grin. While the customer was still in awe, the tea seller had already moved on to entertain his next zealous patron.

In the neighbouring stall, hot *vadas* and *bondas* were being scooped out of a large black kadai. The nimble hands manning the stall was a banian-clad, pot-bellied, middle-aged man expertly tapping the broad ladle with holes to let excess oil drip before transferring the yummy fare on to the plate of his loyal clientele. I would have been tempted if not for this hot, muggy weather; the temperature could be easily around 39 or 40 degree Celsius. I was sweating profusely and trying to get some relief by fanning myself with a handkerchief. All I could do to distract myself was to watch the neighbourhood scenes unfold.

What was I thinking dressing up in a silk salwar kameez that I reserved only for special occasions? What did I even think this was going to be like? Was I expecting to be greeted cordially into an air-conditioned office and given a fountain pen on a platter for me to sign the papers?

We couldn't go and wait anywhere else either because you never know when they'd call, and god forbid we missed it, then another appointment and another day wasted to repeat the same awful waiting process. Famished from the heat and dust, I was almost on the verge of losing it when around 4:30 p.m., Naveen hurriedly signalled us to come inside; we rushed into the official's cubicle.

We were given a look-over, our names cross-checked, a scribble of signature and we were done! Done! All this excruciating wait for this! Two working, professional, tax-paying and law-abiding citizens had applied for leave from work to spend the whole day sitting idle, waiting for their names to be called.

I made a mental note to get my dress dry-cleaned as god knows, I had been plopping down anywhere and everywhere this whole day – on steps, walkways, under a tree and just about anywhere. After a point, I couldn't care less because my body had given up.

Naveen walked up to us and told us beamingly what a successful day it had been and how quickly we had got things done. *Quickly?* I wondered fumingly. But after hearing him narrate the details of how long it usually took for this procedure, sometimes days on end, I realised that today had actually been a huge blessing. I went from complaining mode to full-on gratitude mode in an instant, and that was the power of a government office's experience.

Naveen excused himself and came back in a couple of minutes after enquiring about our next appointment date. He candidly explained all the behind-the-scenes work he had to do to get the work done. We did witness him running pillar to post getting photocopies of documents and whatever else was needed and working his charm all day during our wait, making sure we were as least inconvenienced as possible. Government officials were like gods who decided whether your papers were worth having their initials on or to make you wait for a few more days, just for some comic relief.

I rejoiced a little too soon. The document pushed to the next table was just one step forward. Horror of horrors, looked like the show wasn't over yet! The papers had to move a couple of more tables before our work got done! Damn!

Naveen asked Mani if this was my first time in a government office. I was a little embarrassed that my naivety got exposed so I tried to redeem myself by narrating about my visits to government offices during my student days. That was a lifetime ago and I was probably expecting things to be better, but I had set myself up for disappointment.

A few weeks later, we were back again. This time around, I made sure I wore my most comfortable cotton wear and also took some work along with me and got a pretty good amount of work done by the time our names were called. The day was spent running to the notary public, getting documents typed on stamp papers and photocopied and generally catering to the demands of the officials. In all of this, Naveen proved to be a real gentleman; we were becoming good friends.

***

June 2016

The first thing I did once we got the official documents in hand was to name our farm. Though I'd have liked to narrate a fascinating tale or two on how I came upon the name, but sadly, there was none. Not going to lie, the name 'Kalpavriksha' just popped up into my head instantly. I knew it didn't sound even remotely exciting, but that was the truth. I always liked that name and according to ancient Hindu mythology, the word Kalpavriksha meant a 'divine wish-fulfilling tree'; it was just too good for me to pass it up. Mythology aside, in Sanskrit, coconut palm is considered as 'Kalpavriksha', meaning 'the tree that provides for all the necessities of life'. What better name than that and an apt one for our farm!

Now that the naming was done, we had a lot to figure out. Fencing, electricity and water-supply for the farm were some of the most basic things that needed to be put in place to set our farm dream going. Buying the farm land itself was a bit of a stretch for us and though I fancied a brick wall boundary, one check on the price range for any type of concrete structure made us scramble towards the basic wire fencing.

On second thoughts, I did have this vision to line the periphery of the farm with bamboos and bougainvillea, creating a living fence, and a wire fencing fit into that vision quite seamlessly. With that settled, we immediately started looking for a good supplier and found a local manufacturing unit nearby. A couple of visits to the unit and a few quotations later, the fencing was in place. Along with that, we put up a gate and a plaque with the farm name inscribed beautifully on it.

"I can't believe we got the fencing and gate done so quickly. It really feels like our place now, doesn't it?" I was beaming with happiness, standing outside the gate leading up to our farm.

"It sure does." Mani smiled, running his fingers over the granite stone signboard.

Naveen had given us a heads-up that getting electricity supply wouldn't be easy. By then, we knew pretty well that anything involving a government department surely meant a long-drawn process. Dealing with the electricity board wasn't going to be any different.

Meanwhile, we decided to go ahead with setting up a borewell first to take care of the water needs while we waited for the electricity connection. This took us some time to figure out, given the different options available in the market. There were submersible and surface mountable models and we needed to do some research to better understand which would suit our needs. I left it to Mani to handle the reading and finding the right person for this job. The submersible one turned out to be the best choice for us given its efficiency, low maintenance and less intrusion in terms of noise level and space consumption.

Between Google and talking to the neighbourhood people, we found a vendor to set up a borewell for us. After inquiring around, we found that the nearby bores had water at less than fifty feet. We were advised to go for a nine-inch bore and were told that a manual drill would suffice as the drilling depth was not much. With not much experience in this line of work, we decided to go with the advice. Work started bright and early and after a few observations on how deep the ground water was in this particular area, the workmen got to their job.

It turned out to be a laborious process and we began to feel sorry for the workers. Six hours later, after drilling for about ten feet, the men hit rocks and rubble. We needed alternate options. Further discussions led us to decide on a twelve-inch bore for about 150 feet and to use a power rig drilling machine this time.

The next day, we arrived on the farm early. The drilling team arrived on time with machinery and the work started as per schedule. The supervisor and the driller went around the spot carefully looking at the previous day's work and making their observations. Once they were satisfied with the borewell selection point, they set the drilling rig. The drilling started thunderously, boring into the ground, spewing mud around the perimeter of the hole.

Mani and I moved away from debris and under a shady palm tree to watch from a safe distance. While the drilling was in progress, the supervisor carefully watched for any changes at every foot as they went deeper and deeper. I was told that he was keeping an eye out for silt or boulders during drilling as they would require special drilling pipes. The deafening sounds continued with intermittent breaks to check and report the status.

The rig was so powerful that within a couple of hours, they dug up more than a hundred feet and then suddenly, something about the air changed. I got the whiff of a pleasant, musky scent; the smell of wet earth filling the space slowly. It was something similar to petrichor, albeit without the rains.

There it was, a sudden gush of water spurting out unexpectedly; as if a hidden spring had been discovered. We jumped up and start squealing like school children. What a delightful sight! We were thrilled to bits to see the water gushing out. The sweltering heat of an exceptionally hot June afternoon suddenly became bearable, even quite enjoyable, I'd say.

In what seemed like a very short period of time, the borewell was successfully set up. The machinery, and the people who came along with it, started leaving the farm, leaving us standing there marvelling at this new addition.

Our farm caretaker Velu was rambling on about the borewell and water capacity and such but I had tuned him out completely. I was mesmerised by this contraption. Velu had been taking care of the land before we bought it and we decided to let him continue working for us.

This was going to provide the elixir of life to my future garden. It would soon be time for planting crops, or so I thought.

Our excitement didn't last long. The initial elation of the borewell gave way to the disappointing realisation that the wait for electricity supply was going to be longer than we anticipated; way... too... long. A year and a half, to be exact!

Chapter 4

December 2016

"Have you noticed that there are no worms to be found in brinjals and ladyfingers anymore?" I quipped observantly as I sliced the brinjals for sambar. The glossy, purple brinjals with their mossy green crowns looked almost flawless as I cut them length-wise. I was glancing at the picture-perfect green bhindi sceptically, as they sat on the counter, waiting to be chopped next. I realised in that moment that somewhere I had stopped scrutinising these vegetables for worms as maniacally as I did before.

"And that's a problem because...?" Mani looked puzzled as he peeled oranges and packed our snack boxes. It was 6:30 in the morning and the kitchen was bustling with activity. All the four burners on the stove were fully engaged with a cooker hissing loudly, ready to blow off steam; milk whooshing up to a boil and threatening to spill over on another; vegetables searing and sizzling at the back burner while the mustard seasoning splutters in a pan on another stove.

I was a bundle of nervous energy, zig-zagging from one thing to another – sometimes chopping, sometimes stirring, sometimes grabbing a finished dish and dashing out to place it on the dining table right outside the kitchen, because there was hardly a square inch of empty space on the kitchen counter during this hurdling session in the mornings.

"Of course, it's a problem! Don't you see? Where do you think all the pests suddenly vanished off to? I remembered having to discard a handful of these veggies because they had worms in them. As squeamish as it made me, it was comforting to know that if the worms survived in the vegetable, then it was definitely safe for us to eat.

"But now, I hardly see any. It's because of all the pesticides and poison they treat vegetable crops with! I don't even feel like pushing kids to eat their vegetables anymore! How can I say that when I don't even know what kind of poisonous chemicals they have sprayed on these vegetables? It's so disturbing, you know!" I ranted exasperatingly.

"Hmm... I see," Mani said, nodding apprehensively.

"These food industries are going to kill us all in the name of food, I tell you. I am so furious at this system and all of us who let this go on without blinking an eyelid. How can we just turn a blind eye? How come no one sees this as a problem? Looks like humans are on a suicidal mission. So stupid we are! Tell me which moderately intelligent species would poison itself?" I said, seething with anger.

"We have no option but to buy these! So don't get worked up over things you can't control. You worry so much about these things, K." He tried in vain to pacify me.

I took a quick peek at the clock and yelped, increasing my pace of work. I noticed that this quirky little clock with an 'omelette in a pan' design with a spoon and fork for the hour and minute needle, always made me chuckle even amidst all the craziness. Now, I had come to appreciate it, not for the functionality or the aesthetics but for how it augmented momentary smiles even during demanding times like such mornings.

In getting the breakfast and lunch ready simultaneously, it was a full circus we managed every day. I juggled way too many balls in the air making sure none dropped while Mani walked the tight rope, balancing everything with his sous-cheffing. As the clock ticked, the mayhem rose to a feverish pitch.

The clanging and cluttering of pans increased in volume along with our voices, screaming instructions at M and P alternatively. It was like an orchestra leading up to the finale; what started off melodically in a slow harmonic motion gathered momentum and dramatically progressed towards a crescendo. The atmosphere was rife with tension and then, it all came to an end suddenly with a shattering silence, as I wiped the river of sweat flowing down my temples on the sleeve of my nightdress.

I looked at Mani with a red face, clammy and flush with the thick heat of the growing morning. That pause was a signal to indicate that the cooking part had come to a finish. As the sambar came to a boil, I instructed Mani to watch over it and switch it off in about three minutes.

I carried the steaming hot rice to the dining table on my way out and sat down under the fan for a quick breather. The aroma of sambar boiling and the starchiness of steamed rice floating in the air, blending in and out, orchestrated by the gusts of wind created by the whirling fan bringing in sometimes a mild whiff and sometimes an intense aroma.

I wanted to linger a minute longer, but couldn't. I had less than fifteen minutes to grab a shower, get ready and get to school before the first bell went off. As I walked hurriedly towards the bathroom, I played the agenda for the day in my head, preparing mentally for the morning assembly schedule and the staff meeting planned for the later part of the day.

As I came back into the living room all dressed up, grabbing my ID card in one hand and my wristwatch in another, I was greeted by an empty dining room.

The few moments of bliss under the shower were all gone and my tension returned as I hollered, "Why isn't anyone at the breakfast table? M, where are you? Come here *right* now and have your breakfast, it's getting late. You will have to stand in the late-comers line again if you don't hurry up," I called out impatiently, my voice thundering across the hallway.

Mani was making *dosa* and placing them on three plates for each of us. Once I left the kitchen with the main dishes all cooked, he took over. In all these years, we have slipped into this routine of knowing who takes charge of what, without ever planning or discussing it.

He made sure each of our lunch boxes were packed and ready; and on days like today when it was dosa for breakfast, he made them as each of us landed at the dining table. He didn't have to leave for his office until 9:30 a.m. and that was a blessing we didn't take lightly.

The days when he had to travel out of town for work, were the ones that scared the bejesus out of me and that had been happening pretty often these days. As he climbed up the corporate ladder, his responsibilities had increased manifold too and traveling had become inevitable as he took on a senior position. The silver lining was that the school was within the apartment complex and just a stone's throw away. Therefore, we had one less thing to worry about!

"Put *down* the Tinkle book and wear your shoes, will you, P?" I said gobbling up a morsel of dosa that had gone soggy by now.

"I'm making one more for you, K," Mani said peeping out of the kitchen.

"No, no, I am done," I replied hurriedly, picking up the plate to walk over to check on P.

"I will get him ready," Mani said putting an arm over my shoulder gesturing me to sit down. "Now, will you sit down and have your breakfast in peace? You have about seven minutes to spare. Relax," he said purposefully in a calming tone, making me slow down and breathe easier. With that, he made P sit on a bamboo stool next to him and helped him with his socks and shoes.

"P, you are old enough to do it yourself now. How long will you expect someone to do it for you?" I said crossly.

But P got away by making pleading puppy eyes at his dad and Mani winked at me to let it slide.

"It's okay, I'll do it today. He'll do it himself from tomorrow, won't you, P?" Mani said smilingly at him.

"But Daddy, I don't like putting it on by myself..." P whined in a sing-songy tone still engrossed in his storybook. As Mani slipped the socks on, he called out to M and I saw her stumbling out of her room with her heavy school bag. I saw her peering through her bag and adjusting the books.

As I returned my attention back to my plate, my eyes stopped at the sight of three lunch bags neatly kept near the foyer for us to grab it as we left the house. I felt a sudden surge of relief wash over me.

I know what a herculean task it was to pack lunch boxes, snacks, water bottles, napkins and spoons for everyone, especially packing different snack/juice as per each of our preferences. With me cooking and Mani packing, we had perfected our roles over the years; we sure made a good team. I smiled, feeling a wave of tenderness towards Mani, watching him intently tying P's shoelaces.

This mellow emotion of fondness was rudely interrupted as M let out a loud screech, "Where's my geometry box? I need it today and it's nowhere to be found. I am sure this boy must have taken it! He is always getting into my things. You better find it and give it right now, P, or else!" She stomped over to him furiously.

Let's say we handled the crisis, fed M a few morsels of food and managed to get ourselves out into the elevator just in time as my neighbour got in with her kids in tow. Mani handed me the house keys and we waved at him as the lift door closed. I was lugging two book bags that were bursting with bundles of answer scripts, a handbag, a jute folder and a lunch bag.

I flashed a quick smile at Nancy who was eyeing me with a concerned look as I juggled all the bags and barely manage to mouth the words 'good morning'. M was bent over, tying her shoelaces as the elevator descended. I gave the kids a look-over, letting out a short sigh of relief; thank god the uniforms had been ironed the previous day. Nothing stripped the reputation of a teacher than her kids walking around in school with crumpled uniform and untidy shoes.

We quickly waved goodbye to our neighbours as we rushed out of the elevator and made a run towards the car. I was already dreading the lack of parking space as I was late by a couple of minutes. I ended up circling the school road twice before finding a parking spot and entered the school gates just as the first bell started ringing. Made it just in time. Phew!

***

The morning conversation returned and looped inside my head as I settled down in my room after three consecutive teaching periods. "...but we have no option but to buy these..."

Mani's words echoed. I wondered at our helplessness; helpless enough to buy poison in the name of food.

I was so frustrated with all the running around and earning money to afford the good things in life when I couldn't even provide safe food for my family. What good was all that money then? There just had to be a way out!

Now that we had a farm, what if I could grow all the veggies myself?

There was that thought again, only now, the urge to grow my own food was becoming stronger by the day. The desire to be self-sufficient in my food needs and to not depend on the stores for their pesticide-drenched produce was compelling. How wonderful it would be to surround myself with a beautiful vegetable garden, cook farm fresh meals and spend my time tending the garden. The idea of growing food, cooking nourishing meals and leading a simple, wholesome and fulfilling life was something I dreamt of quite often nowadays.

The satisfaction of feeding my family totally organic, seasonal produce was immense. Reading about losing almost 93 percent of our biodiversity and our native indigenous crops to hybrid invasion was painful. I mean, it physically hurt to think of it; my heart was heavy.

I wondered how ignorant we have been, to have reached this point knowing very well how the precious heirloom varieties were most suited for our bodies, with the unparalleled nutritional value they provided. How foolish could the human race be to think we were progressing?

With every development we seemed to be disregarding nature and its ways; we were destroying its delicate balance and depleting the natural resources. Development seems like an oxymoron as for every one step forward, we were taking two steps backward at the same time.

As I read more, I saw many more disturbing articles, publications and research papers on the horrid details of chemical farming and how it was introduced to the gullible farmers. The more I read, the more I got upset, angry and furious at the system; at the world we lived in; at the way the whole system was being played up by a handful of powerful people while the rest of the population had literally no say or worse, had no idea, about what was happening right under their noses.

My passion to grow food was now fuelled by the desire to opt-out of this deceitful system. The disturbing ugly side of the food industry and how we seemed to have no choice but to buy whatever was sold to us was igniting my passion day by day. When I choose to grow my own food, I'd have full control of what I sowed, what I reaped, what I cooked and what I fed my family.

There would be absolutely no room for doubt and just thinking about it gave me immense satisfaction. In a world where in the name of development and advancement, we were running farther and farther away from nature, poisoning our own food and destroying the ecosystem we lived in – there was a serious need to change our way of life. I desperately hoped that we could slow down just a bit and get back to our roots.

That day, during my biology class, I threw an open question to the class, asking how many would like to consider farming as their career option. I knew the outcome to that question, but just had to know what our next generation thought about it.

As expected, not a single hand went up in favour! Instead, I got shocked responses and amused looks. Everyone was up for becoming a doctor, engineer, astrophysicist and everything else under the sun, but not a farmer. Made me wonder... when did farming become the most deplored occupation?

Was there anything we could do to change that perspective and help create a better outlook about it for our next generation? Could we even think of such a thing as producing our own food? In all these years of depending on the grocery store, was it doable? These were some of the many questions I was asking myself lately.

Chapter 5

January 2017

"You have your Carnatic music class today, M." I saw the phone message in the music group as I walked inside the house, back from school. "Freshen up, have your snack and get ready soon," I called out as I dropped my bags. I finished scrolling through the rest of the messages on my phone and walked towards the kitchen to empty my lunch bag.

"Mummy, not today please." I heard M saying in a whiny tone from her room.

"Why? You already missed the last two classes. Shubha aunty is going to be very upset if you miss today's class as well," I said with mock annoyance.

"But I have many assignments to complete and I also have a class test tomorrow," M's voice droned on.

"Are you even interested in the music classes, M?" I asked abruptly.

"Of course I am. I just don't have the time, Mummy."

She continued, "You know how it is to get the group activities completed, don't you? It is such a pain to get the boys in my group to submit their part of the assignment. They never keep the deadline and I end up having to chase everyone so I can compile the work and submit it on time.

"Because of them, our whole group suffers. I don't want to lose marks for late submission. I hate group activities! Why can't we just have individual activities where we are responsible for just our work? In group activities we get penalised for the delays made by those lazy boys. Why should we have to suffer for their mistake,Mummy? It's so unfair!" M ranted out her frustration.

These were the instances when I was caught between being a mother and being a teacher. Though as a mother, I thoroughly sympathised with her, I explained it from a teacher's perspective. "I understand your frustration, M, but group activities are designed to help you develop soft skills like collaboration, team work and leadership skills; all of which you will need in the real world," I said, sounding like a broken record.

M sulked and carried on with her work. We have had this conversation umpteen times till now. This had been our usual banter on the new assessment pattern brought in by the CBSE boards.

"How about you take a break from the music classes for a while. You do seem to have a lot on your plate with your board exams and everything," I asked gently.

"Can I? But I do like my music classes, it's just that I am not able to practice as much as I want to nowadays. Shubha aunty wants us to practice for at least an hour every day, but I am not able to. I don't want to show up for class without practicing. It feels awful."

Hmm... so this is why she has been reluctant to go for her classes. This one is a perfectionist and as much as I don't want her to be one, it seems like she already is on the road to becoming one.

"Okay then. Let me talk to her and explain that you will be taking a break till your exams get over. At least it will spare me from giving her excuses every week for your absence," I said rather smugly.

"Mummy, you know I am not just making an excuse for

not attending classes, right? I really like them," M said in a defensive tone.

"I know, I know. Don't worry about it. We can resume your classes after the exams," I pacified her.

She got busy with her school work and I went to the kitchen to make a cup of tea for myself. As I tried to find my crooked little utensil to make tea, I wondered where P was and what he was up to. I hadn't heard a peep from him since we all got back from school.

And just then I heard the rhythmic thud of the cricket ball bouncing against the wall from P's room, making it very clear that he was in his cricketing zone. P had gotten rather obsessed with cricket lately; he ate, slept, breathed and dreamt of cricket these days.

As the tea brewed, my mind wandered off to the time when M was about seven years old and P was an itty-bitty three-year-old. I had enrolled M in a Bharatanatyam class that was happening in the apartment complex we used to live in then. A very accomplished master used to take class on the terrace for the kids and I wanted M to have the experience of this art form.

About three months into it, one day after practice,

"Mummy, I hate the *aramandi* practice. I don't want to go to Bharatanatyam class anymore," M declared as she entered the house fussing and fuming after her dance class. Aramandi is one of most important and most difficult postures where the knees are bent and the heels must almost touch each other, the toes must be opened out sideways, so that a straight line is formed by the dancer's feet.

I had been expecting this response from her for quite some time now, but rejoiced at the thought that she stuck it out for three months before she called it quits. I kind of knew this wasn't her thing, but I didn't want to leave it to my own assumptions. What if I was wrong and ruined the chances of grooming the next Bharatanatyam sensation!

Okay, not exactly sensation, but I just had to enrol her to give her an exposure to the dance form. I wanted *her* to decide whether she liked it or not. This was right after we landed in Chennai after our decade long stint in the US. I had decided early on to simply let the kids taste a varied platter of experiences and let them decide for themselves.

On the contrary, little P seemed to thoroughly enjoy the western dance class we enrolled him in. He couldn't wait to get to his weekly class which was about fifteen minutes away from our place. He took to it quite naturally. We'd take an auto to his classes every week.

I had to take M along, as I couldn't leave her home alone. She would pack her drawing notebook or her favourite storybook for the one hour we would spend after dropping him in the class, and wait outside in the park area till the classes got over.

He actually stuck to the sessions and ran the full course until the big finale of a grand onstage performance was organised by the dance school. Ah, what joy it was to see him on stage, strutting about with jazzy clothes, makeup and gel in his hair... oh yeah gel!

The unsuccessful attempt to make spikes out of his springy curls turned out to be impossible as we tried our best. All of three years, P was utterly confused and disappointed at why his hair wouldn't stick out straight-up like spikes. Poor guy!

Since then, there had been karate, art, craft, vocal music, guitar, cricket, keyboard, football and many such hobby classes coming and going in their lives. Some they stuck to, some were dropped off like hot potatoes, which was fine. The only rule we had was, they had to enjoy whatever they chose.

I hated the idea of children hopping from one after-school activity to another, which seemed to be the norm. I got a lot of unsolicited advice and up-turned noses from so-called well-wishers, scoffing and even berating me for not enrolling mine in as many 'enriching' activities as possible.

I decided I wasn't going to do that. Kids were better off spending the afternoons as they pleased, instead of spending an hour doing something they didn't like. The idea of free, unstructured play time was something I liked and we stuck to it.

Our house was always filled with books and our favourite pastime was reading, visiting libraries or parks and of course cooking together. No matter how small our house was, we always had one thing in abundance – shelves and boxes overflowing with books!

That day, I was once again reminded of the purpose of these extra-curricular activities. They had to add joy, not stress to one's life. And I was happy M took the call to take a break from her music classes for the time being. As I sipped my tea, I heard a faint musical note floating in...

S r g m | p, | g m || p , , ,| p , |, , ||
G m p d | n d | p m || g m p – g | m g | r s ||

M was practicing *sarali varisai*. 'She has such a beautiful voice,' I smiled to myself. But before I could finish that thought, my mind went – 'Am I not pushing her enough to pursue and perfect her craft? What if I am hindering her potential by being too accommodative?' There went my brain working against me again, but this time around, I knew better! One thing about M was that if she wanted to learn something, she would double down on it at a feverish pitch. I knew she would get to this later if she wanted to.

But for now, it could wait. Childhood was way too precious to be wasted on talent-acquiring, brain-enhancing pursuits. It must be spent skipping, hopping, idling and daydreaming. And that's how I intended to keep it.

***

In the last couple of weeks, my frustration regarding not being able to start my farm project reached its threshold, as I started doubting whether I could ever do anything concrete on my farm or is my dream going to remain just that – a dream. I was not able to progress any further with my plans because getting electricity connection for our farm kept getting delayed beyond our expectations. It had been over a year and a half now, and this had halted all my plans of proceeding any further.

I was so fed up of waiting around for things to fall into place that I started thinking of what else I could be doing instead of waiting. I started using this time to research about things I needed to know about farming and to try to get as much information as possible on building a sustainable farm and connecting with like-minded people

Just as that thought crossed my mind, almost immediately, as if by some serendipitous synchronicity, things started falling in place. As I started researching more and more, I came across events and workshops regarding farming and sustainable living.

Soon, I found myself connecting with people who had similar interests. A random connection ended up in meeting the farmer in person and touring his farmland, sharing his knowledge on sustainable agriculture.

Another friend who supplied organic vegetables and groceries let us in on the importance of organic sugar, organic milk, cold pressed oil and native seeds. Slowly but steadily, new pathways emerged and the learning and the mind-set shift started happening. My calling towards this life strengthened and my faith in it reaffirmed. Each event, each workshop, and each interaction added valuable components to the knowledge I was seeking.

As I was engrossed in reading an article on circular economy, an advertisement on organic farming workshop popped up on my screen. I was determined to get my family to attend this with me, but I was quite apprehensive about approaching them. I knew Mani would downright say he didn't have time for it and would want me to attend it by myself.

But I knew deep down that I needed to get my family involved in it if I wanted to make it work. The changes I wanted to make in our lifestyle and thinking couldn't happen if I was the only one having all these experiences. So, I somehow pleaded, cajoled and convinced Mani to come along and once he was onboard, I slowly opened the topic of involving the kids in this event too.

He gave me a glare and I could clearly see the disbelief and sarcasm in his look that said, 'You are joking, right?' Convincing a teen and a pre-teen that a two-day organic farming event was going to be the most fun thing they'd ever do on a weekend, was next to impossible. And my two darlings were not your average kids who would just say, 'Okay mommy, whatever you say'. God had given me these two precious spirited souls who challenged every norm there ever was.

"But why, Mom? Why do we have to do it?"

My whole parenting journey so far has been about answering their 'but whys' as much as humanly possible.

I wanted to ask too, but why god, why? Why couldn't we just say, "Because I said so" and move on! So, as one can imagine, it was definitely an uphill task, but I had to try. Mani wasn't even ready to get bloodied in this battle which he was sure we were going to lose anyway, but I went on and on about how this was so important for the kids to understand that he finally, reluctantly, agreed.

We played some reverse psychology, good cop-bad cop routine and what not. It took a lot of drama and quite a scream fest before we packed them up kicking and screaming, and rolled out for the session.

For the record, not that I want to brag or anything but everyone, even the kids ended up having a great time, though they'd never admit to it even at gun point!

Each experience opened my eyes to the wonders of our natural habitat and how beautifully other species co-existed in harmony with each other. The intricate balance of nature and the interconnectedness among various species interacting so incredibly efficiently, without needing to interfere with our existing ecosystems, was mesmerising.

Chapter 6

The more I explored, the more I received. Though it was taking a long while for the electricity connection, in hindsight, I realised that this period was proving to be a golden time. It gave me the much-needed space to delve deeper into all the aspects that needed attending to. It connected me to all the missing links.

I think the universe was testing me if I was truly ready. You don't get what you want just by wishing. The universe knows what you need and gives it to you only if you prove worthy of receiving it.

Meanwhile, there was another thought that had been ruminating in my mind. Would I be happy living on the farm in a little village away from the city? Right off the bat, I knew that I wouldn't want to live a completely off-grid life. I liked city life too much to abandon it completely, but I also liked the idea of a homesteading lifestyle. The paradox of this sounded rather confusing to me.

I kept wondering where I'd fit in. I had seen people called to live an off-grid life and doing just that and then, there were people who were happy living the maddening rush of a city life. I had always found people on both spectrums, either drawn to the rural life or the urban, but never someone hanging in between, like me.

I hadn't figured out where I belonged in this boxed category, and for some reason, it distressed me. I needed to fit in somewhere.

As I went inwards time and again for answers, I suddenly came upon an interesting point – *Do I even have to choose between the two? Why can't I have both? Why do I have to give up either?*

That was when it clicked. This need to fit in was the problem! During that intense internal debate with myself, it dawned on me that I didn't have to choose. Not choosing was a choice too. I decided to stop trying to fit into a box. I decided to create my own category; wait no, rather not fall into any category at all. And that was liberating!

Living in a city with proximity to my farm and doing what I liked without worrying about the stereotype of how a farmer should or shouldn't be. And in that moment, a heavy load sort of lifted off my mind. It was so freeing! I felt lighter. That's when I realized that these societal shackles that seem to keep us bound and caged, exist in the realm of our own minds as much as they exist outside of us. Sometimes, we are just a thought away from breaking free.

***

An article on the Green Revolution caught my attention as I settled down with my laptop after wrapping up kitchen chores post dinner. The kids were in their respective rooms and Mani was watching cricket reruns on TV. As I delved into the topic, the ugly side of this whole exercise made its appearance. Every link took me deeper into disturbing details, leaving me baffled. Each layer peeled off exposing one malicious intent after another.

How did I never come across this before? The menacing connection between the end of WWII and the beginning of Green Revolution, that propagated increased usage of fertilisers and pesticides, was too much of a coincidence. Then came the hybrid invasion and the seed monopoly exercised by the industry giants; the fight for farmer's right to save seeds and the legal case being fought for decades to ensure that the farmers have the right to save their own seeds. All this made me exasperated.

How in the world was this even happening? Was the general public even aware of these outrageous atrocities? Were we as consumers so gullible that we didn't even seem to know things happening around us? Who was responsible for all this? Who decided what the rest of the human population got to eat? We were poisoning our own food, water and air! How was this development? How could we call this advancement?

I read fervently about regenerative agriculture, natural farming and permaculture. I understood the ethics of farming more and more deeply.

From-scratch, home-cooked meals were slowly disappearing and making way for the readymade, ready-to-order meals. There was something so fulfilling and nourishing about a farm-to-table meal that we hardly ever get from the supermarkets we shop from. In this rat race and mechanised life, somehow as a society we seemed to be veering towards the fast-food life which may fill our stomachs, but did not provide the nutrition our body needed for a healthy life.

***

> *"When you want something, the whole universe conspires to make it happen..."*
>
> — Paulo Coelho

This season in my life had made me believe in this quote. Once you started listening to your inner calling and made room for your passion, the universe conspires to make things happen for you, but not before testing your worthiness to deserve it. Whether you called it the Law of Attraction or any philosophical mumbo-jumbo, all I had to say was it's true!

In what I could call random dots that appeared out of nowhere and then connected with one another, here I was in a bustling metropolitan, working a regular job and dreaming about living in a quaint little farmhouse surrounded by fruit trees and flowering shrubs, growing organic vegetables on my farm, which was located some forty kilometres away from the city limits. How was this even happening?

I didn't know if it's the universe conspiring or it was Google baba playing the universe card by throwing up the right things my way! I'd never know, but I was going to take these as signs from the universe.

Somewhere in the middle of all this, I had started experiencing an inner turmoil of wanting to quit my job to concentrate fully on my farm. This feeling seemed to appear completely out-of-the-blue and started consuming me almost immediately. I didn't see any rationale in it, except the pull was getting stronger and stronger with each day. I wanted to discuss this with Mani, but I didn't find proper words, explanation or any proper reasoning to support my decision.

Every time I tried broaching this topic, it sounded so frivolous and absurd to me that I changed my mind about discussing it. I had been silently mulling over it for over a couple of months, keeping it a secret within me. No one knew about this quiet uproar brewing in the dark confines of my heart, especially with no clarity in sight of the 'why' or 'what' of it. I finally decided to spring it upon the unsuspecting soul on a dewy November morning during our walk.

"The weather is so pleasant today, isn't it?" Mani said stretching his arms over his head.

I nodded noticing the slight nip in the air that morning but my mind was preoccupied.

"Hey, before I forget, let me tell you that I'll have to travel to Mumbai in a couple of days. The travel itinerary isn't finalised yet, but I wanted to keep you posted. Let's finish the grocery shopping tomorrow, just in case."

"I am thinking of quitting my job," I blurted out suddenly.

"Huh?"

"Yeah, I have been thinking about it a lot lately."

"Is there a problem at work? Why the sudden decision?" Mani seemed perplexed.

"Oh, no no... it has nothing to do with work. It's just that..." I scrambled for the right words to describe what was on my mind. It sounded stupid, now that I thought about it.

"Didn't you tell me that you are being considered for the post of Assistant Vice-Principal next year?"

"Yes, and it is HUGE! I mean, such a remarkable recognition and opportunity. To be chosen for this promotion among such talented and experienced hands around, is nothing short of amazing!"

"So?" Mani probed further.

"Lately, I am feeling this strong pull towards wanting to develop our farm and to start growing vegetables and fruits for our needs; to live a life closer to nature, you know. I am not able to shake off this feeling somehow.

"I keep thinking that it's just a temporary fetish of sorts and it will go away with time, but it doesn't seem to. I have been thinking about it for three months now and I seriously don't know what to make of it."

"Hmm..." Mani nodded, absorbing it all.

"What do you think? I know it's sudden and does sound like a rash decision to make when everything is going spectacularly well. Who in their right mind would throw away a golden opportunity at work like this, right?" I peered at his face, looking for his reaction.

Now that I had spoken the words out, this whole thought process sounded totally crazy, not to mention utterly irresponsible of me. To leave a well-paying, reliable job with an upcoming promotion to add on, and for what? Growing vegetables? It didn't sound sensible even to me, leave alone its making sense to anyone else.

I had a job that I loved, lived within the school campus and all of us had comfortably settled into the routine. Just when I thought I was all ready to retire from this job at the ripe old age of sixty, I was confronted with a decision that would turn my life 360 degrees.

I was on the cross roads with one road well-laid out, smooth and shiny, promising me more than I ever aspired for, and the other, beckoning me towards a less travelled one, muddled with no clear pathway in sight.

"It definitely looks like you have given it a lot of thought. I agree with all your points, but it's ultimately your decision to make," Mani said with his characteristic sensibility on display.

"You are not helping one bit," I said frowning.

"Look, K, you did make a very clear pros and cons list and all I can say is, give a good thinking through once again. But once you're done, go with whatever you decide. Finally, the call has to be yours."

There was no way to explain this unrelenting feeling. It was so strong that I couldn't take my mind off it. Man, this was something else! I hadn't experienced anything like it before. I really couldn't explain it to someone who hadn't felt that way.

This strange pull, I didn't know what to call it, but I was unable to escape it. This definitely must have been what passion or calling is! That was why it didn't make any sense to me.

It was vexing me to be torn between my love for teaching and this calling to till the soil, to grow a garden. I often found myself daydreaming; smiling, muttering and pondering along with a quiet realisation that this figment of my imagination that was running wild could not meet reality.

But could it?

Chapter 7

Take the safest route; decide with the logical part of your head; don't take risk – all the sane advice I had received in my four decades of lifetime had gone haywire as I decided to go with my heart.

When I told Mani, he smiled – a smile in which I saw sympathy for my naiveté that screamed 'what the hell are you doing?' but also, there was a quiet reassurance that whispered 'go ahead, I got your back'.

My overthinking self was used to doubting my decisions and always looked over to Mani for any major decision making, but this time around, I was oddly determined. Or was I just helpless at the hands of my passion? I'd never know, but I had to do this despite my best judgement.

When the decision fatigue had set in, the final straw for me was to imagine what it would feel like if I continued with my job. I panicked at the thought of *not* loving something I had loved doing for so long, and if I stayed in the job for the sake of all the logical reasoning, I might end up being miserable. And that did it.

The day to submit the continuation letter was getting closer and I knew what I had to do. When the day arrived, my principal and mentor summoned me for a meeting; a meeting I was dreading. With that started a series of changes; I truly started fully accepting the fact that I really was taking the plunge. That was when it started sinking in.

***

December 2017

"What? What do you mean, Velu *ayya*?" Mani seemed shocked. Mani was in the balcony inspecting the plants when he got a call from our farm caretaker. I was prepping for lunch and overlooking P's homework at the dining table when his elevated pitch grabbed my attention.

"What happened?" I said getting up to walk towards him.

Mani gestured to me to wait and moved further towards the balcony, listening intently to what was being said.

"When did this happen?" I heard him saying. I went back to my carrots and beans, wondering what it was all about, as I watched over P working on his science homework.

"Always label the diagram neatly on the right-hand side. How many times have I told you this?" I reprimanded him.

"Mummy... please! This is good enough. I don't want to redo this."

"Oh no, you are not submitting this shabby work. Come on, erase the labelling and write it again. It'll hardly take a minute and you'll see how neat it looks then. Your science teacher will definitely give you a star for this," I cajoled him as he rolled his eyes and reluctantly pulled out his eraser.

I returned my gaze towards Mani and found him looking puzzled at whatever Velu ayya was narrating to him. Our caretaker had a knack for wrapping simple information into mini bombshells and dropping them on us. In the last year and a half, we had come to know of his flair for drama. He'd start the conversation with the most bizarre piece of information without the head or the tail of it.

Along with this flair, he had a *drinking* habit which added to the drama quotient. To figure out whether he was sober or not was a task in itself when we spoke to him over the phone. We had kept him working for us due to consideration for his old age. It always took a bit of probing on our part to get him to the point and then we'd see what an inane subject matter it was. Nevertheless, he got us flustered without fail every single time.

I finally resigned to the fact that this was probably one such episode.

A couple of minutes later, Mani disconnected the call and looked at me beaming ear-to-ear. I looked on quizzically, wanting to know what the hullabaloo was all about.

"Guess what? We are finally getting the electricity connection for the farm!" Mani declared jubilantly.

"Wait, what?" I almost fell off my chair. "When did this happen?" I was still not sure I heard him right.

"It's happening as we speak," he said without missing a beat.

"I have been dying for this moment, but you can't spring it upon me like that! It takes many a few moments to sink in. I'm still in shock. This is huge!"

"I couldn't infer much from what Velu was saying. He was going around in circles and his speech was slurred because of 'you know what' so I gave up probing him further. We need to go to the farm right away to get the full picture," Mani said, already hurrying up to get ready.

"You mean now?" By the time I looked around, Mani was nowhere in sight.

Ten minutes later, we were driving over to the farm with kids in tow, where the people from the electricity board were already setting up the post. I didn't remember the drive; it just seemed like we got teleported to the farm all of a sudden.

By the time we arrived, the electric post had been erected and the workers were winding up the work. That post next to our farm entrance was the most beautiful thing I had laid my eyes on. This was the beginning of that elusive dream I had been nurturing for so long. If this wasn't a sign from beyond, then what was?

***

Procuring the electricity connection catapulted me into a frenzy of 'what next' because I hadn't anticipated this coming so suddenly. There were no signs of it and then one day 'boom', there it was! All this time I had been blaming the lack of electricity for not being able to do much and now that it was there, I was paralysed into inaction.

I had to overcome the analysis-paralysis if I wanted to get things moving. I was definitely gearing up to use every opportunity to get out there and learn whatever I could. But being an introvert, I had my own limitations in getting out of my comfort zone. Then again, it wasn't a dream if it didn't push you over the edge and made you do unbelievable things.

I saw myself signing up for every event/workshop/session on gardening; meeting organic farmers at farmers markets, visiting organic fairs and exhibitions on weekends. This was how my new schedule looked like. I was absorbing, documenting, researching and making my own blue-print for my farm. But now that I had to put all of this into action, I was stuck.

***

As I started visualising being on the farm and doing the things I wanted to, I started noticing a lot of gaps in my planning. I realised that just having a piece of land and knowing how to garden wasn't going to cut it.

"We need to build a small tool shed? You know, we will need a space to keep all the miscellaneous farm stuff, don't you think?" I said as I drew the map of the farm on my notebook.

Mani nodded and went back to his laptop and his work. I continued working on the map, filling in details of where the vegetable patch would be and where I wanted the trees to be planted.

An hour later, Mani gave me a 'what were you saying' look as he glanced at the sketch I was working on. As I explained and we discussed further, more issues cropped up that we hadn't even considered.

"Once we start the gardening work, don't you think we'll be spending a lot more time on the farm? In that case, we will be needing more than just a tool shed," Mani said.

Looks like we hadn't thought through enough. My heart sank a bit, thinking of all the possible issues we need to address before we took the next step.

"We need a place to rest too. If we plan on working on the farm on the weekends, we need a room to cool off, a restroom obviously and a make-shift kitchen for a quick cup of tea maybe," he added.

Of course! We'll be there every weekend for sure. With both of us working full-time jobs in the city, (I still had four months left before I would be officially relieved from my school duties) we would be able to go to the farm only on weekends.

"That means we will be needing a caretaker for watering the plants during the weekdays? So, we need to look at hiring an extra farm helper," I was thinking aloud.

With these questions poking their heads, all the excitement vanished into thin air. The path looked bleak and disillusionment returned. We were back to square one.

What was I even thinking? That I could just start a little garden and live off the land just like that? Who did I think I was to have this audacious dream in the first place?

Maybe this was a crazy idea to begin with at this point in our lives. Maybe we should hold off this project and revisit it post our retirement.

I recalled the meeting with my principal and mentor. Sitting across from them and discussing my resignation was one of the most difficult things I had to do. But the funniest thing happened. While I was talking in all earnestness and seriousness, they weren't taking my decision seriously at all. They didn't seem to be convinced by what I was saying. They brushed it aside to momentary frustration caused due to overload of work and started discussing how they could reduce my workload.

In their defence, I guess decades in this service had made them see the month of December to be of peak frustration among the staff members and they were used to receiving many resignations of which most never materialised. This was that time of the year when everyone nurtured a rosy picture of resigning and chilling at home with a glass of their favourite beverage.

Staffrooms were bereft with every other teacher ranting about the work-load and throwing around the 'R' word left, right and centre. That was the general mood around this time. So, they were sure it was my frustration speaking. I even noticed my mentor hinting at my principal to lay off the topic for now and that I would come around soon.

Basically, they dismissed my plans of resignation, no matter how serious I was. After that first meeting, with every encounter it was becoming more and more obvious that they hadn't mentally accepted my resignation, and this was distressing me because I was dead serious about it and they weren't.

***

So, everything seemed to be indicating that this wasn't the time for my farm dream. Maybe I should revisit it post my retirement. Few days went by in utter desolation and then, a sort of crazy thought crossed our minds.

What if we went ahead with a farmhouse project first and held the vegetable garden project off for a while?

It sounded strange and exciting at first! Wow, a farmhouse! Could we? Wouldn't that be amazing. But wait, where was the budget for it? The more we thought about it, the more it became clear that without a place to stay, the garden project would never work out.

Because truth be told, an organic farm without a house was a disaster waiting to happen. Initially in our excitement, we might be willing to brave the scorching sun (summers can be killer down south) and the rains, but not for long. Without a place to rest, we knew we would eventually give up. And that's not what I wanted. We needed a sustainable, long-term plan.

Chapter 8

With electricity on our farm and the quiet realisation of the necessity to build a farmhouse, my mind was on overdrive; I dove head-long into designing my cosy farmhouse, scrounging books and the internet for farmhouse ideas and that pretty much seemed to be the order of the day of late.

Of course, we weren't naïve to not notice the big financial crunch this would put us through. After running through a lot of ideas on how to fund the construction, we decided that a bank loan and selling the plot on Raja street (where I initially dreamt of growing vegetables) was the only way to take this forward.

Long story short, building a farmhouse was added on into the grand vision for my farm. Initially, I panicked and didn't think we should stretch ourselves thin. Mani sat me down and explained in detail how we could go about it starting with securing a loan to flag off the project and in the meantime, find a buyer for the city plot we had.

His self-assured way of running me through the details instantly put me at ease. It made sense to sell that property which was at a prime residential location in the city. This would help us not only in financing the farmhouse construction, but also ease our tight string budget on the rest of the farm maintenance activities.

That part being looked into, our next big question was to find a builder who would suit our budget and sensibilities.

After one meeting with our prospective contractor, we were totally convinced that he was the one for us. He understood our financial constraints and kept allowance for the outrageous ideas I put forth too. He was related to Naveen and knowing him from the time of finalising the farm property, gave us the comfort to sign him up for the farmhouse deal. Once we shook hands on that, things started moving pretty fast.

Once we brainstormed ideas and the vision I had for the farmhouse, the ball started rolling and gathered great momentum in a short time. I started having all kinds of beautiful farmhouse dreams! From just wanting a tin-shed, we were now looking at a small two-bedroom duplex.

This new development sent me into rapture; feeling over-the-top excited, anxious and a total nervous wreck, all at the same time. This was a totally unexpected development and there was so much to plan.

I didn't know where to start. From designing the farmhouse look – the exterior and the interiors, the elevation, the doors and windows to tiles and wall paint – it all seemed too overwhelming. But it was also a beautiful time of grand imaginations. Devouring beautiful farmhouse pictures, searching the internet, and designing my own little cottage started occupying a lot of my mind space. So, with the enlightenment for the need of a house on the farm, the journey ahead became clearer.

As the idea of a cottage started taking shape, I decided I might as well go for the kind of look I wanted as long as I stayed within the budget. Once the plan of a farmhouse really started to sink in, I was thrown into the confusion of million different beautiful options there were for a farmhouse.

I suddenly found myself enfolded with expectation galore to follow the traditional *Chettinad* style house with its inimitable *Athangudi* tiles, iron-pillared *nadumuttam* and the quintessential front porch *thinnai* and all the works.

Though I loved those heritage style houses, I once again went against the popular advice, threw caution to the wind and decided that I wanted a Santorini style blue and white cottage. Given the small space that we were going to be using for our house, I decided to marry my western style sensibilities with eastern functionality and came up with a fusion design. Who says you have to stick to one or the other?

Style is personal and shouldn't be based on others' ideas or approval. I had a few other ideas I was particular about and I was sure to try my best to get them all incorporated.

One thing I always wanted was a swinging back door from the kitchen that would open into my vegetable garden. I had this dream vision in my mind of me pushing open the swinging door and walking into my kitchen with a basket of freshly plucked vegetables for lunch. This recurring daydream was the ultimate farm dream and I had to make it happen.

Having huge windows all over the living area would lead to a seamless feel of the outdoors even while we're inside was another very specific requirement I had. I wanted the sunlight streaming in from all directions and I wanted to be able to see the trees and the vegetable garden while I cooked. I wanted the kitchen sink to be placed right where it would overlook the backyard garden, so I could see my garden even while washing dishes. Clearly audacious dreaming!

I wished to have an open island kitchen which wasn't separate from the living area. The intention was to create a very cosy feel without a lot of partitions. Once the design and aesthetics were in place, we spent a whole day at the digital design centre explaining our vision. The next few weeks went by in choosing the type of tiles and wall paints.

Our builder, Vishal, was a thorough planner and made us pick-out all the things we needed for the house at the very start so the work could go on seamlessly and we didn't have to go back and forth to shop for things at the nick of time. A brick-finish accent wall grabbed my fancy and I tried to get my contractor to see if he could fit that into our budget.

I was very fortunate to have a builder who was patient with all my multiple iterations and still kept a straight face, occasionally even sharing a bit of my enthusiasm and suggesting some new variations. He took care of all the technicalities and kept it very simple for us to navigate the whole process.

We also had to be very meticulous about the electrical and plumbing points early on to avoid modifications later. With all the nitty-gritties sorted, the farmhouse construction started in full swing.

While the farmhouse construction was going on, I couldn't sit idle so I started planning my vegetable garden space and started looking at the positioning of the sun and watering facilities. Not being able to do anything on ground, I did the next best thing; something I was good at and something that I always do before any big project – a 'Brain-dump' activity. Basically dumping all my ideas on to a paper and getting it out of my head. This always helped sort things and gave me better clarity. I rolled out a big sheet of paper, grabbed a few markers of different colours and drew up a blue print of my raised beds for the vegetable garden.

I first marked out the periphery with specific trees that were meant to serve a specific purpose; some were to serve as biological pest control, some as nitrogen-fixers and some would act as wind-breakers. I chose castor, sesbania and bamboo. Next, I marked the areas for the compost pits.

This was planned to provide constant supply of nourishment to the vegetable patch. I then worked on the raised beds and carefully worked on what was to be planted in each patch marking along the companion plants.

I pulled out all my notes that I had meticulously prepared over months and referred to them, as I marked the spaces on the paper. Once I marked clear rows for vegetables and herbs, I created a timeline of events leading up to the sowing season in July. At the time when I was planning all of this, it was late January. Well, you could never be too early planning things, I suppose.

Chapter 9

Seeing me buried in these charts and stationery supplies, Mani rolled his eyes, wondering if I had lost my mind; he just didn't say it in so many words but he made it quite evident.

"What's all this?" he remarked casually, trying to look as nonchalant as possible seeing me occupy the whole dining table with stationery supplies strewn across every inch of the space.

"Well, I am planning out our raised beds. Didn't we decide we wanted to build raised beds for our vegetable patch?" I said.

"Yes, we did, but it's only the end of January for crying out loud and the sowing season is only in July! We have more than five months!"

As if I had been waiting for him to ask me that question, I directed him to go through the blue-print and the time-line of activities I had been working on so far. He was a man of few words and wanted short and quick answers to his questions. He couldn't be bothered with elaborate descriptions and so he was visibly miffed when he got a huge list to go through instead of a short reply.

Sitting down reluctantly, he heaved a big sigh eyeing the TV remote in his hand longingly. He had made up his mind that this was a ridiculous exercise and that I was wasting his precious TV time. With half-hearted interest, ready to pooh-pooh it all with one glance, he eyed the doodles on the paper. I showed him a break-up of the work plan written out in my 'brown diary' listing the activities month by month, leading up to July.

February:

- *Find neighbourhood resources to hire tractor, JCB, manure, etc.*
- *Calculate the surface area and arrive at the number of trees that can be accommodated in that space.*
- *Identify the sources to purchase organic and native varieties of the tree saplings and vegetable seeds.*
- *Make a list of fruit trees and flowering trees we want to plant.*
- *Identify the locations for each tree plantation.*

March:

- *Hire a tractor to till the land, to uproot all the weeds and loosen the soil.*
- *Sow urad dal (black gram) seeds on the vegetable patch to make the soil nitrogen rich.*
- *Take care of regular irrigation of the patch.*
- *Monitor growth of black gram.*
- *Dig out large pits of 4 ft by 4 ft at identified locations to plant trees, making sure there is minimum 10 ft spacing between tree saplings.*

April:

- *Start plantation of fruit trees by April.*
- *Start experimenting with planting vegetables in small sacks away from the construction site to test the nature of the soil and its fertility.*
- *Start planting bamboos and bougainvillea as live fencing and other border plants.*
- *Attend as many workshops for hands-on experience of organic farming.*
- *Learn more about companion planting.*
- *Learn about the seasons and understand seasonal crops of Tamil Nadu.*

May:

- *Harvest the black gram.*
- *Plough the rest of the plant back into the soil to enrich the soil.*
- *Finish building a compound wall around the vegetable patch.*
- *Purchase native organic seeds for July sowing season.*
- *Order bricks to line the raised beds.*

June:

- *Start working on the raised beds for the vegetable patch.*
- *Collect sugar cane husks from street vendors.*
- *Source a tractor load of cow-dung manure.*
- *Start planting the peripheral border crops for natural pest control.*
- *Start working on seed starters.*

July:

- *Start sowing seeds from second week of July.*
- *Start them in the store room in a dark area.*
- *Prep the seeds – soaking them in water for 8 hours to jump start germination.*
- *Name them and monitor germination.*
- *Once germinated, keep them in indirect sunlight.*
- *Once they are big enough to be transplanted, take it to the farm for transplantation on the raised beds.*

After about fifteen minutes I heard him exclaim loudly, "Oh dear god! We hardly have enough time on our hands!"

"*I know*!" I replied with equal fervour.

I was glad we were on the same page. And I was more than glad that I had done this exercise because if nothing else, I had a solid action plan to fall back on and that brought a lot of relief.

This was why I believed in doing the brain dump activity, because otherwise, multiple things swirling inside my head didn't do much except overwhelm me. I knew there was so much to be done before July, but now I knew exactly what and when it was needed to be done before the sowing season was upon us.

Yes, I might have gone a little overboard with planners and stuff, but that was just me. I always needed a plan of action, couldn't work without it! So writing the plan out in my 'brown diary' (yes, I have one exclusively for farm related stuff) made me breathe easier, and putting things under various timelines gave me a sense of control.

So once we went over the list, Mani was convinced more than me that we better got on with things while the construction was still underway. Though it looked like I had a lot of time on hand, the time-line activity made me realise that I had no time at all. I needed to get started on certain tasks right away.

***

While I couldn't grow anything on my farm yet due to all the construction work, I used the time to learn and record a lot of things at home. From growing vegetables in containers in my balcony garden, observing and writing down the types of pests that attack different vegetables and journaling the details of when to plant, what to plant and how to save seeds were all happening alongside. There were lots of successes and lots of failures too, and I meticulously wrote down every minute detail of everything I tried.

The weekend was arriving and I had a long list of activities planned out for our farm visit.

Chapter 10

I couldn't believe my eyes when I arrived at the farm. There was a riot of machineries and loud, ear-piercing noise! There were huge trenches dug out everywhere. The entire place looked ravaged by giant machines with piles of sand, bricks and mortar strewn everywhere.

It was a jolt to my senses to see my usually empty, peaceful meadow-like farm, turn into this rumbling space bustling with activities. But what else was I expecting to see?

Though I knew this was how it's going to be with all the construction going on, it came as a bit of a rude shock to see the farm in this state for the first time. Within three weeks of commencement of work after the *bhoomipooja*, the foundation work had been going on fairly well.

Mani and I went around the construction area and inspected the work happening with a wide grin on our faces. Things seemed very much in control and were going on at a good pace. We were thoroughly pleased.

***

Back home, my experiments continued. As a science student all my life, I knew a little too much than usual, which was a curse sometimes, because you just couldn't live in your bubble of 'ignorance is bliss'. Having a postgraduate degree in life sciences with biotechnology, immunology, biochemistry and microbiology as my major subjects, I was becoming painfully aware of the over-use of pesticides.

I had been coming across numerous articles lately on how our immune system was getting compromised with increase in our daily usage of chemical cleaners and pesticide-laden food consumption. Studies on super-bugs being on the rise due to the over-use and abuse of antibiotics and the pharma industries playing gods had been scaring the wits out of me.

I was now scanning everything I purchased and scrutinised my family's consumption behaviour. A long-forgotten memory popped up in my consciousness while I was in the middle of all of this. I remembered winning an essay-writing competition in my undergrad and had received a set of three books as my prize. One of them was about the harmful chemicals that were found in everyday cosmetics and toiletries.

This was way back in the nineties, long before the parabens and sulphates were exposed. It was one of my earliest memories of coming across the hazards of commercial products before the chemical contamination became rampant. It also had a compilation of simple homemade alternatives to shampoos, soaps and face packs using natural ingredients. I loved that book and became very fond of trying out the homemade *ubtan* recipes it provided. Now to think about it, I guess it did have an impact on me early on.

Soon enough, I signed up for a day-long soap-making workshop which seemed like a god-send to me because it wasn't common at that time to find such workshops happening around the city. By then I was totally convinced that I wanted to make my own soaps and was fervently looking to learn. Skin literally absorbed everything we put on it, and soaps were something we used every day.

Reading the fine print of ingredients in store-bought soaps and the medley of incomprehensible chemicals used in them made me a determined soap-maker. Initially it was a lot of hassle to procure the raw materials and the equipment required for soap making. I had to run pillar to post trying to source the best materials, and then it took me another few weeks to start having the confidence to do it myself. It took a lot of dedicated time and effort to master the art of making soap, but I finally did it.

I realised that making my own soaps was the only way I could control what went into the soaps my family used. Once I discovered the joy of soap-making, there was no stopping me. I was loving my experiments with homemade soaps.

It opened up another avenue for my creative juices to flow. The various permutations and combinations, the designs, the flexibility to customise my soaps with my choice of wonderful skin nourishing ingredients, soon became an addictive hobby.

Here I was, at twelve in the night on a working day, mixing my soap and waiting for it to trace so I could pour it into moulds. It made me feel like I was witch-crafting and somehow reminded me of the fairy-tale 'Rumpelstiltskin' and the scene where the witch dances around the fire at midnight.

I preferred making soaps at night, so I could give my undivided attention without my kids interrupting me in the middle of it. Soap making had almost completely consumed me. I was concocting designs, fragrances and colour combinations for my creations every waking hour. Such was the obsession!

I suddenly found myself turning into this DIY crazy lady; I was doing things I never imagined I would do in a million years. It was a strange time and I didn't know what was happening to me. Never had I ever imagined that one day, I would be making my own soaps!

Well, neither did I imagine in my wildest dreams that I would become a farmer one day, but here I was, all set to become one! I guess once the homesteading bug bites you, you invariably start doing some pretty crazy stuff; at least crazy according to the society. I was now making homemade natural cleaners too, replacing one commercial cleaner after another.

At work, all my friends who were only privy to my very sensible and diplomatic self, were now raising eyebrows at my new avatar. Who would have ever thought that a seasoned teacher at the threshold of a prestigious promotion, would want to quit everything at the drop of a hat and ride this wild dream of becoming a farmer?

Chapter 11

It was the beginning of March. Spring had arrived and brought with it loads of tender greens, buds and flowers. It was Saturday and as we were driving down to our farm in the early hours of dawn. All around us, fields were painted in hues of green.

As we entered the village, there was a burst of yellow everywhere. The *poovarasan* (portia) tree bloomed gloriously in every household. As we passed through the village, I saw cows resting under trees, leisurely chewing cud; there were children chasing each other blowing on the little flutes made out of the heart-shaped leaves of poovarasan. It instantly took me back to my childhood days, and some forgotten memories flashed through.

I recalled the times during my school days when I had visited my ancestral village with my family during my summer vacation. We'd roll the leaves on our palms and make mini-cigarette-like things and blow through them, making loud, sharp, startling sounds, and giggle all the way to the fields. It was an everyday affair in those few days that we spent there. It was our instant DIY toy to play and make music with.

The sweet scent of frangipani flowers filled the air as I pushed open the gates to my farm. The sudden hit of that fragrance was intoxicating. I strolled mindlessly towards the scent and it led me to where I had planted it. There were lots of blooms and a few buds as I stood there soaking in the scent.

I had imagined it would come up as a small tree and look nice and dainty on the sides of the driveway. But to my utter shock it had forked out into four branches from the base and had now spread rather like a bush instead. It seems to have a mind of its own and had spread its branches into the driveway and looked like it would soon become a hindrance to the pathway. But I tried to push the thought aside and focused on enjoying its beauty. I dropped my bags beside me and sat down by the driveway.

The construction site looked forlorn and empty, but soon the place would be buzzing with activity. There would be rumbling machinery, JCB at work, and the cement mixer churning out fresh mixture to be plastered on the walls and floors of the structure that was coming up. The house had already taken a substantial shape. It was amazing to see a huge cement structure in the middle of the farm now.

My eyes that were accustomed to seeing an open space with grass and weeds with only a sprinkling of coconut trees here and there, were finding it difficult to adjust to this new imagery. Within weeks, the scenery had changed drastically. I still couldn't believe I was witnessing all of this; was it really happening? I was afraid I'd wake up any minute and realise that it had all been just a dream.

"Ma'am, ma'am?" I was a bit startled to hear Vishal. I got up to meet him and saw the steady stream of workers pick up their equipment and walk towards the construction site. The day's work had begun.

***

It was P's birthday month and he was an early planner. By early I mean, he started planning his birthday one year in advance. This year was going to be extra special as he was entering his teens. Oh my, what a sea of change this number brings.

To see my little cuddly baby grow into a toddler and then a pre-schooler and finally now a teenager was not something I was able to get accustomed to. All the other stages before this had not seemed this alarming, but this number 13 sure made one sit up and take notice.

I realised quite suddenly that the little guy who would always sit literally pressed against me, squishing me, even though there was a lot of space on the sofa, now sat at a comfortable distance from me. All these years spent, nudging him gently away from me so I could have some breathing space, but now I had all the space I wanted... and yet I was hurt. I wonder why? Sigh!

The little boy who would narrate all about his school and sports team in great detail without stopping for a breather, now only answered in nods and 'hmms'. I dared not persist any further or else I' be rewarded with dramatic sighs, grunts and eye rolls in abundance. And anytime I talked nostalgically about the action figures and toys he used to love, he gave me a look as if I were a basket case.

All the tight hugs and kisses were dwindling and becoming rare, and any physical display of affection was a strict no-no. I was amazed at how grown up he suddenly seemed one moment and how child-like the very next minute.

There were moments when he came into the kitchen and put his arms around my waist and told me he loved me and quickly disappeared before I even realised what had happened; or when after a tough hour spent to help him complete a difficult project or assignment, he slipped in a heartfelt thank you; and when after a particularly hard meltdown, he walked in minutes later to quietly apologise with sadness written all over his face.

In all those unexpected moments, I was caught unaware and got a glimpse of that little soul hiding behind the teen facade. I wanted to bottle up all those moments somewhere safe so they didn't fade away in my memory.

With all that the year 13 was bringing in, there were those rare moments when he incessantly talked about that cricket match he had played, and explained animatedly about how he was holding the bat, how he hit the ball, and how the ball went flying and he scored a six; that's when I got to relive those past years of the jolly carefree childhood years which he was slowly leaving behind, and trying awkwardly to embrace adolescence while trying his best to deal with the bouts of emotions that he didn't quite understand, but still wanted to show that he was grown up enough to handle things on his own.

I was preparing myself for all of this, because no matter how difficult this phase might be, I still didn't want to forget any part of this. It was an important milestone and like all the others that came and went, this one would come and go too. I knew that I'd blink and it would be gone. So, I was here to cherish the moments.

As I planned his birthday, my mind wandered off to a time just a couple of years ago.

"Hey, come on, P? Time for bed," I called out from the hallway as I went about switching off the lights and saw him still busy playing in his room.

"Mummy, two more minutes?"

"No, come right now! It's getting late. You..." Before I could finish my sentence, I sensed a swift movement and it was P racing past me to get to the bed first.

"Hey, don't run..." I said and heard him chuckling loudly as he plonked himself on the bed. As I walked towards the bed, he pulled the blanket over him and covered himself head to toe into a bundle and rolled up to the middle of the bed. I wondered for a second what was happening and then realised what he was up to!

Every night we'd tell him to move to one side of the bed, but he wanted to sleep only in the middle, right between the two of us! I was totally fine with the arrangement except that this guy gave some deathly kicks in the middle of the night which sent me reeling in pain while in deep sleep. To stop him from occupying the centre space, we tried rushing to the bed and leaving only the side spot for him. He must have noticed what we were doing and so he took his revenge!

He mumbled from inside the covers, "I am a cocoon now, and you can't make me move." You see, once he was a cocoon, it was clearly a lost cause. It meant he had marked his territory and would be sleeping right in the middle of the bed between me and Mani, and it was up to me to safeguard myself with some extra pillows and cushions. I tried very hard not to laugh and kept my voice stern telling him to move to the side, knowing well that it was a lost battle.

Usually I would get a little miffed at this antic of his, but that night as I saw him jiggling inside that blanket still laughing triumphantly, I was overwhelmed with love. I hugged the bundle that he was and happy tears threatened to trickle. I wanted to enjoy this moment, this innocence, and this unbridled show of affection!

Mani caught my eyes with a questioning look. I just smiled. He attempted to cajole P into moving to the side of the bed, but I signalled to him not to. That night he slept between us as on most of the days and we hugged him as we drifted off to sleep.

And in the present, as I recalled the above incident, tears stung my eyes. How the days were flying by. I wanted to hold on tight to these fleeting years. I knew this phase would be gone before I knew it. And, therefore, no matter how messy these adolescent years might be, I didn't want to let them pass me by like a blimp.

This phase called for a more nuanced kind of love because it was not going to be easy. I had seen that with M. Loving them when they say they hate you, and loving them when their friends take precedence ripped your heart. I would have to be extra loving when things got tough. At the end of the day, I will be the only one who will love them for who they are, no matter what! And they need to know that.

Chapter 12

Back home in my balcony, I had all my grow bags and pots readied with potting mix and I had sowed some of the vegetable seeds. I had been monitoring their growth and recording my learning meticulously. But apart from the experimentations with growing my veggies and dreaming about the farmhouse, there were others things occupying my time.

Funny things start to happen when you start thinking about organic farming. It was not just the quality of produce I started questioning, but basically everything around me. I was manically reading the labels of practically everything that entered my house.

I was sceptical of the packaged food, the cleaners, and all the personal care items. Low and behold, just as suspected, I found everything alarming.

But what could I do with that information? What good were all my findings if I couldn't do anything about it! And then the frustration started to set in. I frantically searched for alternatives to replace these and realised how much as a family we had come to depend on the neighbourhood supermarkets.

Over the years we had come to rely upon them heavily for everything, and that made me painfully aware of how little control I had over what I consumed if I were to just mindlessly buy what was sold to me.

This was another huge turning point in what I considered my journey towards a more sustainable and self-sufficient life. Though I thought I'd been living as consciously as possible, this made me take a closer look. This period marked my silent resolution to intentionally start making efforts to cut down my dependency on the grocery stores.

I had started eyeing all the packaged food we bought from stores very suspiciously, and every time. I read the labels, I would swallow hard. I'd google the incomprehensible contents on those labels to understand what they really were and how safe were they for consumption. I had been feeling quite disturbed about the processed food items we purchased and bread was one such item on the top of my list which was giving me sleepless nights because it was the oft-bought processed food on our grocery list.

After browsing the internet for 'how to bake bread at home', and failing miserably many times, finally I gave in to the temptation of investing in a bread-maker. Now, the funniest part was I didn't even know there existed such a thing as a bread-maker. Being quite an adventurous cook, I prided myself in knowing most of the culinary appliances but this I didn't know! But when I did come across it, I was immediately sceptical about its utility.

Well, it was quite an expense to simply take a chance with it and the cynic in me needed to know if it was worth it. After extensive research on lots of bread-maker brands, I finally bought one. Thus began my experimentation with baking my own bread and making homemade jam and cutting out processed food one item at a time.

"Mmm, I smell something good! What's cooking, Mummy?" P walked into the kitchen inquisitively.

"I am baking bread," I said smiling at him.

I fell in love with the aroma and freshness of homemade bread, and there was no way I was going back to the industrial bread available on the racks of the grocery store. Once you have baked your own bread, you will never go back to the store-bought one. It was that addictive.

What a revelation it had been to know that we could actually consume freshly baked homemade bread at home! The experience of freshly baked bread was something we all fell head-over-heels in love with; it was love at first smell!

Ah finally, we bid farewell to the industrial bread; no more worries about preservatives, acidity regulators, 'permissible' flavours etc., etc.

Homemade bread recipe

Ingredients:

- *2/3 cup lukewarm water*
- *1/4 cup lukewarm milk*
- *2 tablespoons butter*
- *2 1/2 cups flour*
- *5 teaspoons sugar*
- *1 1/4 teaspoons salt*
- *1 teaspoon active dry yeast or instant yeast*

Procedure:

Place the yeast and sugar in a large bowl and stir in the warm water and wait until everything is dissolved. Add in warm milk, butter/oil and the salt, then stir in the flour. Once it all comes together, transfer the dough on to a clean surface and knead well. The dough we are looking to create must be soft and pliable, not too sticky.

Knead on a lightly floured surface or in the bowl itself, for 6 to 8 minutes, or until the dough is smooth and elastic.

Place the dough back in the bowl and cover with a kitchen towel. Allow it to rise for about an hour, or until doubled in size.

Once that's done, beat the dough down and place it in a lightly greased loaf pan and cover it to let it rise in it.

Meanwhile, preheat the oven to 375-degree F (180 degree Celsius).

Pop the loaf pan in the oven for 25-30 minutes or until golden brown.

Allow it to cool on a wire rack completely before serving.

For best results, rest the bread for 4-6 hours before slicing.

And of course, once you started making your own bread, how could you slather it with the gummy store-bought jam? Absolutely not and so, the other things followed. I started making my own jam, butter, pasta, ketchup, burger buns and even cheese at times, which I never thought I would be making at home. I wondered why it never occurred to me before to try all of this. Anyway, better late than never!

It never stopped here. Lots of other things followed too.

***

"Mani, look here! I found some great pictures on Pinterest for the pergola entrance I wanted, and look how cute this lily pond looks! We had been talking about this the other day, remember? I have saved some pictures; come I'll show you."

I was super excited as I brought the laptop out and plopped next to him on the sofa.

"Ooh, and look at this one! This is too good, don't you think! Hope Vishal could build this little pond within our budget?" I kept rambling on, wondering why Mani wasn't saying anything. I glanced over and see him furiously typing away on his laptop with eyes squinting and eyebrows dangerously knit. That was usually the sign to back off. So, I decided to wait.

After what seemed like a very long time, Mani peered at my laptop screen for a second and said,

"K, listen, go ahead and choose what you think is best. I am really tied-up with some serious client deliverable issues. There are multiple showstopper concerns I am dealing with right now. Between client meets, proposal presentations and my travel plans, I don't think I can spend much time on this.

"The next couple of weeks are going to be tough. I have back-to-back conference calls throughout the day and then there are team meetings that might not leave me with any time to provide inputs on farm related decisions. It's going to be really hectic for at least a month, if not more. Remember, the farm project is your baby."

"You need to call the shots. I'll be okay with whatever you choose, so go ahead with your decisions," Mani's voice trailed off as he went back to his laptop screen.

"But..." I saw how swamped he was with work. And at that exact moment it hit me, that he was absolutely right! This *was* my baby indeed. This was *my* dream project and even though I had painted quite a vivid picture for Mani, he still had no clue about the vision I had for this space.

I would have to stop badgering him for suggestions on every little thing. I needed to take the calls myself on things I wanted to get done. Except for the major decisions, I would have to learn to take the shots myself.

With the farmhouse construction added on to my little farm dream, this project had grown so much bigger than what I initially had in mind. It was not just about creating a small vegetable garden anymore, but something above and beyond my wildest dreams. This definitely needed single-minded focus and some serious planning and execution; and that's exactly what I'd have to give it!

This whole thing about being the sole in-charge of the farm happenings started sinking in. It surely made a lot more sense and made things more streamlined and clearer. The decisions got made quicker and I stepped up to taking an active part in everything farm-related.

Up until now, we had gotten into the pattern of me telling Mani what I wanted done and then him taking it up with the men involved at work, whether it was our builder, construction workers or farm-helpers.

The men on the farm too felt at ease approaching Mani for everything. I guess it all boiled down to the general mentality we harbour in a patriarchal society that we lived in. I went along with it as it was just easier that way.

But I guess, if you needed things to change, *you* needed to change. Taking up the lion's share of the decision-making surely made things easier on Mani, who couldn't be bothered with minor details, while it also helped me immensely to be able to work according to my pace.

Chapter 13

At the farm, Mani and I went around inspecting the work. We took different routes around the construction area and met-up at the starting point with a big smile on our faces. I could already envision my blue and white cottage somewhere in the midst of all the construction debris and rubble. Things were moving at a steady pace.

While there, I went to the far end of the plot and took a look at the proposed vegetable patch. The first thing that came to my mind after examining the patch was that it needed a lot of work before anything could be grown there. The land was sparsely covered with parched brown grass and dry thorny shrubs.

The soil condition seemed very poor and barely had any life in it. That's where I had to start then; first thing was to improve the soil fertility before doing anything else.

I had planned on sowing black gram (*urad dal*) as a nitrogen fixing crop in the soil as a first step. Once the crop matured, I planned on ploughing it all back into the soil to add green manure and help build the organic content of the soil. This had to be done immediately as it would take three months for the crops to mature, giving us enough time to prepare the land and start making raised beds before the sowing season in July. We barely had enough time to get things in order.

While the construction was happening, we decided to work on the areas away from it that didn't come in the direct line of workers or machineries. That way we could maximise our time and get the farm ready for plantation by the time it was sowing season. I also wanted to start off planting tree saplings as early as possible because it would take them a long time to grow.

Reading and researching on plants had become an important ritual for me by now. It was during one of these times that I came across an extraordinary book called *The Hidden Life of Trees* by Peter Wohlleben. It opened up a whole new world for me and changed the way I looked at trees.

The way we humans thought of the plant kingdom, and how it actually functioned in reality, were so far off. To learn that trees too lived as families and that they communicated with each other, and had unique ways to assist other fellow plants during distress, blew my mind!

The author talked about how scientists found that neighbouring trees helped each other by feeding, through their root systems either directly by intertwining their roots, or indirectly, by growing fungal networks around the roots that serve as a sort of extended nervous system connecting other trees. He wrote,

Trees live in symbiosis with hyphae (fungus/mould roots). A teaspoon of dirt contains kilometres of these roots. One species can spread throughout entire forests over centuries. They exchange nutrients with trees, along with information about insects, drought and other dangers. It's like a 'wood wide web'.

I knew how intelligent each creation on our earth was, but to see this level of brilliance in plant species was mindboggling. I was a changed person. I couldn't look at trees the same way I had before. I was someone who has always been in awe of plants and this new dimension of knowing them deepened my fascination for these mighty creatures even more.

***

I pulled out my carefully researched data of regional trees. I had been compiling an extensive list of tree species knowing the importance of indigenous plants in the survival of other local fauna of the region. I compared it with the list of flowering trees that I had written down that attracted birds and butterflies.

I had come to understand that birds had very distinctive nesting habits. They were very particular about nesting only on select native trees.

Butterflies too had very specific host plants they preferred. So, it became very important then that I carefully picked and chose which trees to plant in the limited space we had. I had to eliminate all the huge trees from the list due to space constraint and narrow down to small and medium sized trees only.

The trick lay in understanding which trees met the needs of the regional birds adequately and prioritised them. I needed a clear picture of exactly how many of those trees I could accommodate on my farm.

I took a look at my notes to go through it a final time;

Trees that attract birds:

- *Fig varieties top the list of trees that attract birds.*
- *Mango trees are said to attract Golden Orioles.*
- *Cherry trees attract koyals.*
- *Red Silk tree attracts parakeets.*
- *Indian Coral Tree is a hot favourite of birds.*
- *Hibiscus, Parijatham and Tacoma attract nectar-drinking birds such as sunbirds.*
- *Mynahs roost in Mast trees (Ashoka trees).*
- *The Rain tree is rated high on the list of bird attracting trees. It's said that the bark of a rain tree teems with insects,*

beckoning birds to flock to these trees for feeding, roosting and nesting. (But I can't have it as it's a huge tree and we don't have that kind of space.)

- *Some of the common species of trees that attracts birds are Lagerstroemia, Gul mohar – Delonix regia, Cassia javanica, Jacaranda...*

Some common indigenous trees which serve as excellent habitats for birds:

- *Mahua Tree (Madhuca longifolia)*
- *Jamun Tree (Syzygium cumini)*
- *Neem Tree (Azadirachta indica)*
- *Mango Tree (Mangifera indica)*
- *Bullet wood Tree (Mimusops elengi)*

I wanted my farm to be a thriving microcosm of ecosystem. And to achieve that I needed to plant more of indigenous trees that would attract the local birds because they recognised regional trees and shrubs as sources of food and shelter. Birds were sceptical about exotic trees that they weren't familiar with.

They were accustomed to local and native plants. As these plants thrived well in their own natural habitat, it seemed like a no-brainer to plant more local varieties than exotic ones. Though I did have my heart set on planting some exotic varieties of flowering trees, I had to let 'em go.

I had been teaching interdependence of plants and animals for so long, but to learn that birds simply won't nest on just any old tree was interesting to note. Those birds were intelligent creatures, I say! I carefully chose plants that produced seeds, berries and nuts that would become food for the birds.

I also chose native flowering plants to feed butterflies, bees and other pollinators. I thought my problems were solved with this research and all I had to do was get these varieties and plant them. But it was easier said than done. Finding the varieties, sourcing and learning which ones really suited my soil was a big hurdle to cross, but we finally zeroed-in on Gul mohar, Cassia marginata, Spathodea, Plumeria, Parijatham and Singapore cherry.

I also kind of worked out a blue-print to indicate where I wanted each tree to be strategically planted; a tall tree near the car park and small ones lining the pathway leading to the car park and such. A mix of big and small trees so their canopies didn't block the sunlight for each other.

With all this information at hand, we charted out a plan for the following week's farm visit.

Plan for the next week:

- *Call Velu ayya to make sure he gets the patch tilled and ready for sowing urad dal.*
- *Inform the builder to have pits dug out for trees using JCB.*
- *Note to self to procure whole black gram seeds from our regular organic vendor.*
- *Pack it along with the things to carry to the farm in the farm bag.*
- *Call local nurseries to check availability of the tree saplings we need.*
- *Visit nurseries on D-day to pick up the tree saplings.*

Yes, we had more than a couple of farm bags specified just for our farm visits. One understood the importance of it after leaving behind crucial stuff back home. When you knew you couldn't drive back home to get it and, therefore, the work you had planned couldn't get done until the next weekend, you learned to pack things extra carefully.

Our once-a-week farm visits were precious and we could never ever forget to pack what was needed for the day.

So, everything was planned out and I was raring to go! I packed the things the day before and kept them in the hallway and set the alarm for 5:30 a.m.

As I got ready for bed, sleep evaded me. I went back to reading some more of the hidden life of trees. As a biology teacher, I had taught children about the food chain and the food web umpteen times, but hadn't actually read a real case study before. Wohlleben took an example of Yellowstone National Park to demonstrate the centrality of trees in the earth's ecosystem.

It all starts with the wolves. Wolves disappeared from Yellowstone, the world's first national park, in the 1920s. When they left, the entire ecosystem changed. Elk herds in the park increased their numbers and began to make quite a meal of the aspens, willows, and cottonwoods that lined the streams. Vegetation declined and animals that depended on the trees left. The wolves were absent for seventy years. When they returned, the elks' languorous browsing days were over. As the wolf packs kept the herds on the move, browsing diminished, and the trees sprang back. The roots of cottonwoods and willows once again stabilized stream banks and slowed the flow of water. This, in turn, created space for animals such as beavers to return. These industrious builders could now find the materials they needed to construct their lodges and raise their families. The animals that depended on the riparian meadows came back, as well. The wolves turned out to be better stewards of the land than people, creating conditions that allowed the trees to grow and exert their influence on the landscape.

I pondered if human civilisation through all the modern developments had only succeeded in completely cutting us off from our natural systems. We couldn't live in isolation in our concrete jungles and continue to destroy the natural ecosystems, yet think we could thrive.

Were we truly that short-sighted to not see the bigger picture of how this interconnectedness was what kept the ball rolling and it was probably our only way of survival? Was this gross inability to see and act in accordance with the grander scheme of things in a universe built on mutual dependency leading us to our doom?

Chapter 14

The alarm rang and we jumped out of bed. Amid the contemplation of the previous night, I don't remember when I fell asleep. We went about exactly as per our plans. I had already bought and packed the black gram the previous day, and so bright and early we set out to visit the nurseries along the way to the farm, to pick up the saplings.

Sowing the patch with a nitrogen fixing leguminous crop and tilling everything back into the soil was something I was going to try from my own theoretical understanding. I somehow felt very strongly about it, even though I hadn't come across any mention of this in any organic gardening resource. The mention of nitrogen fixers had been plenty, but not in the way I was planning to do. I was basically about to put a theoretical concept to action.

I had to first explain it to Mani, and then to Velu. It took some convincing to make him understand why we were doing this. Though Mani was onboard with it, Velu ayya and the farm helpers were perplexed by what I was saying.

They kept convincing me that adding urea and fertiliser was the best way to go. And when I didn't seem to pay heed to that, they simply rolled their eyes and mumbled something among themselves which looked like a mix of contempt and pity for my lack of knowledge in farming.

The absurdity of me, a city dweller trying to *explain* farming practice to villagers who had been doing it their whole lives wasn't lost on me. Especially, when I had zero 'on-ground' experience. Talk about the irony, phew! I knew how cocky I sounded even to myself.

But I also knew that organic farming, though a common ancient practice, had become an alien concept to our farmers of the post WWII era. All they had been used to was chemical farming ever since the day they started practicing it. It was ingrained in their psyche that it was the only profitable way to farm.

So, if I wanted to do things differently, I knew that I'd have to be patient in explaining the 'whys' to them. And as absurd as it may sound, I knew that I had to stand my ground every step of the way going forward to change the way things were done on my piece of land.

I also knew that until they got to see the results for themselves, they were not going to be convinced by my methods and so until that time, I'd have to learn to be okay with their unsavoury reactions.

"*Illa Amma*, it won't work, not to mention it's time-consuming and tedious. Moreover, why would you grow a three-month crop just to plough it back into the soil? You could instead just add urea and start growing your vegetables," Velu ayya tried to reason.

"I know it is a bit of a longer process but I want to fortify the soil naturally without adding any fertiliser. I am trying to grow my produce without any chemicals or pesticides, Ayya," I replied in vain.

"No pesticides either? Oh, you aren't going to harvest any produce then, let me tell you that. The pests won't spare anything. It'll never work. Anyway, it's my duty to warn you, rest is up to you, Amma." He shook his head with disdain written all over his face.

"I know you mean well, Velu ayya, but let me just try my way," I said wanting to put an end to the conversation.

I actually surprised myself by standing my ground and putting my foot down in this particular matter. I did not let anyone dissuade me or allow self-doubt to creep in. I was determined to grow my vegetables purely in an organic manner and nothing was going to stop me from trying.

That day at the farm, I found the patch freshly tilled and ready to sow black gram. For once my old man aka Velu ayya had managed to get the work done as instructed and just in time too, without giving us vague excuses.

His tall-tales were legendary and honestly, I was a bit apprehensive about him finishing the task, but he had pleasantly surprised me. I was excited to get to work. I grabbed the urad dal packet from my bag and proceeded towards the tilled patch. The next hour was spent scattering the seeds on the patch at regular intervals to ensure it was well spread out. Once that was done, we instructed our old man to water the patch as we headed to the next task at hand.

We walked over to the spot where the tree saplings needed to be planted. Vishal had made sure that the 4ft by 4ft pits were dug out as instructed. I went around and counted the number of pits and the number of tree saplings we had with us. The extra farm helpers we had called in for the day's work started arriving and we began by giving out instructions for the work ahead.

We grabbed the sacks of potting mix, red soil and manure that we had kept ready under a make-shift shed. We got the tree saplings and placed them next to the pits they needed to be planted in. I was extra cautious and made sure there was no mix up because it was important to plant them in the right spots. One small mismatch and our whole layout would go for a toss.

There were bigger trees and there were smaller ones. Each had been planned to be placed strategically where there was enough room for it to spread. There were also walkways and pathways that we had designed. So, I personally oversaw the transplanting of each tree sapling and assigned them to the right pit.

It was 9 a.m. by the time we assembled everything and started the process. Along with the workers, we dug, mixed up the soil and manure, carried and planted the saplings and filled up the pits carefully. It was an early February morning, but the sun was already scorching. Down south, it was more or less summer all year long for us. So, if it wasn't physical labour, the heat was definitely wearing us down.

Man, this was hard work. Standing in the sun all day didn't seem to be my cup of tea. I had been mercilessly teased as 'delicate darling' all my life, and I had kind of internalised it over the years. My husband and I were the quintessential city folks used to the sedentary lifestyle with minimal physical activity and air-conditioned environs. This heat was seriously taking a toll on us.

At a particularly weak moment, I started having my doubts whether we were cut out for this weekend farming thing after all! Did I just fall for the romantic idea of a farm life? I was seriously thinking about it. It was 12:30 p.m. and I guess it was time to take a much-needed break inside our air-conditioned car.

The minute we sat down and a whiff of cool air hit our sweaty faces, the realisation of what we had gotten ourselves into dawned on us. We quietly glanced at each other and carefully avoided saying anything. But we knew what was going on in our minds. *What possessed us to venture into this, when we could be at home comfortably chilling in our air conditioned living room, sipping cool refrigerated water? Was it too late to back out now?*

But our thoughts were interrupted by our rumbling stomachs and we quickly diverted our attention to the lunch we had packed. We learnt early on that packing our own lunch was the most sensible thing to do while going to the farm. That way when we were hungry, we weren't wasting time looking for a restaurant half an hour away outside the village.

That little lunch break really helped put things in perspective. A little cool air and a sumptuous lunch helped clear the head. We didn't know how ravenous we were until we finished our lunch; farm work surely worked up quite an appetite and made you appreciate your food.

After a short, well-deserved break, we needed to get back out in the sun. Oh yeah, the items on the to-do list for the day had not been ticked off yet.

We had some planting of vegetable crops and flowering plants to do in small sacks around the space we had chosen away from the construction area. While picking up the tree saplings, I had spotted a few plants I wanted to try growing in the sacks, till our designated raised beds for our vegetable patch were fully ready. This was going to be our trial garden, a warm-up exercise in becoming future gardeners. I had picked chilli, tomato, hibiscus, ixora, jasmine, chrysanthemum, brinjal and basil.

The rest of the afternoon was spent planting these in discarded jute bags and cement bags lying around. It was 4:30 p.m. and we were red in the face, sweating profusely, hair dishevelled, covered in dirt from head to toe and standing dead on our feet. Bone tired yet totally satisfied, I didn't know that was possible. I was expecting to feel dejected by the sheer amount of physical work it took to just be outdoors in the soaring temperature. Half expecting to throw in the towel, I was surprised by my own resilience. I was experiencing an emotion so different from anything I had experienced before.

Sweaty, messy, scraped knuckles and dirt under my fingernails, but instead of feeling miserable I was feeling... content, fulfilled and a sense of accomplishment that I had never felt in a long time.

As we drove back home, I looked at Mani, waiting to hear him complain about all the work, heat and tiredness, but strangely enough, I saw the same contentment on his sun-tanned, smiling face.

Chapter 15

The following weeks required us to do more of all this. We were totally living an alien experience, something our bodies weren't used to. I was someone who would get a migraine at the drop of a hat and would avoid any and all forms of triggers; of which hot temperatures, exposure to scorching sunlight and dehydration were the biggest ones. The days and weeks that followed were filled with all of these and yet it felt like I was living in a trance.

Though we had started planting flowering trees at our farm, fruit trees were still a distant dream as we were waiting to hear from our trusted organic source. I had this little fantasy of sitting under my mango tree with a book and a cup of tea. That was an image that floated around in my mind every once in a while, leaving behind a longing for it.

Finally, about two weeks after we started our tree planting, we got a call that our fruit saplings were ready! I couldn't be happier and had them delivered at our farm immediately. We gave clear instructions to Velu ayya to water the plants regularly until we got there the next weekend.

We advised him quite clearly not to transplant them immediately, as the plants needed time to get acclimatised to the water conditions at the new place for a few days before transplanting. These were the instructions that came from our farmer friend and I was going to adhere to them.

***

Weekends were spent on the farm and weekdays had activities bursting at the seams too. Come Monday and our school routine took over feverishly. Pre-board preparations were going on in full-swing and there was a certain tension in the air for students and teachers alike. Board instructions, rigorous revisions and tests were happening every day.

We were also preparing to distribute the hall tickets and conduct a candle-lighting ceremony for 10th graders; an event signifying a collective prayer and blessing session before they left for their preparatory break. On the other hand, 11th and 12th graders were busy with farewell preparations.

After school, I noticed M in her room, busy at her desk with her school work.

"How are things at school, M?" I asked, as I picked up the lunch bags lying in the living room.

"Thank god, I chose the computer science stream in 11th, mummy. My friends in the biology stream are literally dying under the load of diagrams they have to finish for their record," M said heaving a sigh of relief.

"Hmm, I hope that wasn't the sole reason you chose computer science stream?" I chided mockingly.

"Not really, but it definitely seems now that I took a wise decision," she cackled.

It reminded me of the time when we had gone over the possibilities of choosing a stream, and what a nervous-wreck she had been! About a year back around this time, we had to get into some serious soul-searching in order to pick the right stream after her 10th boards, and for that, we had to get to the bottom of what she really aspired to do after her schooling. It all started with M walking in from school one day, a little flustered.

She dropped her heavy bag down and pulled out one of the dining chairs to sit.

"Mummy, everyone seems to know pretty well what they want to do after their 12th, and so they are very clear about which group to choose after the 10th boards. Looks like I'm the only one who's clueless," she said, visibly annoyed.

"I am sure everyone is going through some confusion at this point, but let's figure out what is it that you want for yourself," I said calmly, trying to make her feel at ease.

"See, this is the problem right there," she said accusatively.

"What do you mean?" I was confused, wondering what I had said wrong.

"All my friends seem to know what they want to do because they *had been told* what to do by their parents constantly since they were little. And I guess, somehow that became their own aspiration too over time."

"Wait, now are you saying—"

M cut me off mid-sentence. "But before you jump at me, I am not saying that's the right thing for parents to do. They shouldn't thrust their wishes on their children... and also for the record, let me make it clear that I am happy you and daddy didn't do that to me, but..." She seemed lost for words.

"But, what?" I probed.

"See, I don't know how to say it. It might sound like I am contradicting my own statement here but I am starting to think that probably it might have helped if you guys had certain specific expectations of me that might have shaped my thoughts towards what I want to pursue." She sounded unsure and utterly confused.

"Do you seriously think that would've been a good idea? By doing something like that, we would have influenced your thoughts and that may not be something *you* genuinely want for yourself. Look, M, I know you don't mean it and you are just saying it out of frustration at the moment.

"And believe me, I totally understand what you are going through. It is a confusing time. It's time to sit and really think about what is it that you want to do."

"And how do I do that?" She looked desolate.

"Work backwards. Think of what kind of work life you envision for yourself? I know it's difficult, but start there. And then based on that, we can think of what you need to take up to get there."

I paused before adding, "I am going to make tea. Do you want some?"

I knew she liked tea. "I'll make your favourite cinnamon tea, okay?" I looked towards her and saw her nodding.

As the tea started brewing, I made sandwiches for the kids' afternoon snack. I turned back to see M walk into the kitchen and slump down next to the refrigerator with her back resting on a cabinet. That was her usual place to sit when she was in the kitchen, talking.

I could see that she had a lot on her mind. While she was highly spirited and spoke her mind, keeping us parents on our toes most of the times, she was also the most level-headed teenager I had ever seen. And believe me, as a high school teacher, I had encountered tons of them.

If I said that she hadn't swayed under peer pressure even during her teen years, then that was saying a lot! Virtues like that were rare and precious. I knew that and appreciated that in her. A lot.

I waited for her to speak. Probing never worked. Always backfired. As I got ready to pour a cup of tea and hand it to her, she started talking.

I listened.

I sat on the kitchen floor facing her as I stretched my legs out and leaned on a cabinet opposite hers.

"I'm very clear that I neither want to do medicine nor engineering, mummy," M said finally.

"Okay, that's a start. But the bigger question isn't what you don't want, but what you *do* want," I replied.

"Hmm... I don't know," she said thoughtfully.

"You are a genius at math and sciences though. Have you considered that?" I had to make sure she wasn't missing something.

"I've thought about it. I enjoy math and physics, but just because I am great at something doesn't mean I have to make a career out of it, you know?" she said it with such confidence that I was stunned. Such clarity of thought at this young age!

I was so impressed by how M thought and articulated herself. She had been that way since a very young age. She knew what she wanted and had such conviction in her thoughts that belied her age.

"I never thought about it that way, M. That's a very good point you made. Also, I really want you to consider your creative talents. Your artistic skill is a god-gifted talent, and I see how happy it makes you," I said and waited for her response.

And we started working backwards as she listed out things envisioning what kind of work-life she aspired to have and what an ideal job felt like for her. The daylight started dimming and the kitchen started getting dark as the sun was about to set. We had been talking for more than a couple of hours now.

"Let's discuss more later once daddy gets home, okay. I am sure you will have more clarity soon." I got up to put the tea cups in the sink and watched M in a contemplative mood. Her mind was on over-drive for sure, but she looked much calmer than before.

Later that night, after a lot of back and forth, loud thinking and discussions, we kind of arrived at some vague outline of what her inclination was towards. Among many other things, a career in design seemed more appealing to her. She had seemed so much more relaxed after that discussion and got enough clarity to decide that she would opt for the computer science stream.

Mani and I on the other hand, knew pretty well that this meant a lot of research work for us as we would be the first ones in our circle to be venturing into this field. And of course, the thought did cross our minds that this would mean dealing with the extended family's reaction when they realised that the choice wasn't either one of the two biggies that they had come to expect of her, given her excellent academic record. Well, we'd get to it when the time came. Right now, it was enough that we had clarity on the stream she had to choose after her 10th.

***

It was almost ten days since the tree saplings arrived at the farm, and that day's main agenda was going to be transplanting these saplings. Just thinking about it made me giddy with happiness.

Pomegranate
Mango
Fig
Black Jamun
Sweet lime
Lemon

Sapota
Guava

These were just a few from our long list of fruit trees. More would be added to the tribe in the coming weeks. In the meantime, we called on some extra farm helpers again on the weekend for the plantation. The pits of 4 ft by 4 ft were already done, and so all we had to do was finish transplanting the fruit tree saplings.

We had the same set of farm helpers this time around too and it was much easier to get things done as they already knew how to go about it. This weekend was all about the fruit trees and we successfully transplanted each one in its designated space. Our knees were dirty, backs were aching but our hearts were full!

Chapter 16

April 2018

At the work front, it was the fag end of the academic year at school, and as teachers, we were busy correcting answer scripts, preparing mark lists and report cards. Staff meetings and syllabus discussions were the norm of the day. Department-wise meetings and level meetings were held to plan the curriculum for the following year.

In all this time, I had many briefings, advice sessions and meetings to help me rethink my resignation. I came out of each of them with a heavy heart and sometimes even on the verge of contemplating my decision. It was a heart-breaking period.

As my notice period came closer, the reality of leaving behind this life started sinking in. I got ready with my handing-over process. My interactions with my friends and colleagues too become more intense and more intentional. I was leaving this institution after nine long years! My association with the school had been since its inception and that made me even more nostalgic.

Every day as I walked into the gates, I started becoming more and more aware that this routine that had become second nature to me, would soon become a thing of the past. And I started becoming very intentional about everything I was so used to and had never given a second thought. Like the elevator and the staircase I used to take to reach my room on the second floor, the corridors I went around on duty, the classrooms, the furniture, the black-board, the chalk box, the playground, the library and everything else.

I savoured the morning assembly, the prayer, the meditation, the school bell after every period, the sounds of squealing kids, the mini lunch time prayer, the announcements that came over the PA system and the evening dispersal routine. It was surely painful to think of leaving behind this place which had so many memories attached and had become my second home!

The days had become quite emotional and most days ended in tear-jerking moments. Almost every day I met my team members, friends and colleagues in small groups or individually. Some who were much older than me, still hadn't given up on convincing me to stay back.

They tried to tell me how fool-hardy my decision was, given the opportunities of growth I'd been presented with. I knew they had my goodwill at heart, and I saw how pained they were and how hard they tried to tell me that this wasn't the best decision.

It pained me to not be able to explain to them why I needed to do this, so most times, I just listened. I took in all the love that was pouring out through their words of concern and tried to bottle them up inside. With others, we reminisced about some wonderful times spent together in the past.

We recalled the times we had to huddle up in the tiny computer centre and finish entering the marks of students in the system, and of times we had shared coffee and snacks during the half days.

Most of these sessions had ended in roaring laughter and some of these laugh riots ended up in tears as well. I knew leaving my job would be hard, but never ever imagined it to be this hard! The out-pouring of love and pleas and advice to not leave was really overwhelming! I kept wondering more often about what I had done to deserve so much love!

If I was not meeting up with my teaching gang, then there were the students who surrounded me. Every break-time and lunch time, I found a group of students waiting outside my room. I shared a room with the headmistress of the school and it was located on the second floor adjacent to the 10-A classroom, and diagonally opposite to the staff room.

Every time I was in my room, I invariably had some student visitors waiting outside to meet me. It broke my heart to talk to them as some got teary-eyed and left me with heartfelt 'we will miss you, ma'am' notes and handwritten cards and letters. Some still hoped that I would change my mind.

I was being given surprise farewells by my students that they organised within their classrooms. The autograph session and the charts filled with loving messages signed by all the students of the class was given periodically by various class groups. Chats and photo sessions followed.

If not for my teachers and students, my mentor and my principal made it even more difficult for me to face them every day. Their love and their expectations from me made me feel like I was betraying them by not changing my decision to stay back.

Most days, when I was walking down a corridor, I found the house-keeping staff dropping their work and gathering around me, taking me by surprise. They enquired in hushed tones whether what they heard was true; whether I was really leaving the job. And when I smiled in acknowledgement, there was an instant look of sadness and shock mixed together.

They wanted to know why, and I soon realised that it was sometimes just easier to tell them that I needed a break; and keep it simple. I came home most days with a heavy heart.

Everyone who knew me and my journey as a teacher thought I was crazy to leave a promising career and a loving team behind. Sometimes, you didn't fully understand why you were pulled towards a particular direction. You may not have words to describe it or even explain it to others, but deep down you know you have to do it.

It would seem so against all your rational judgement. Your logical part of the brain cannot comprehend it, and might even feel perplexed. That's exactly how I felt during that time.

With days passing by in this perpetual state, I finally faced the LWD – last working day – and I was surprised to see that many of my colleagues were still shocked to know I was serious about my resignation. Somewhere they had been under the impression that eventually I'd change my mind.

As I was walking with my colleagues towards the conference hall for the customary team lunch, my mentor grabbed my hand and took me into her room for a quick talk. She pulled out the sacred ledger showing my credentials that I had earned over the past nine years. It was a record book of employees and their performance, and my name ranked number one on the list.

She didn't say anything. She just gestured towards it and threw a glance at me that said, "Do you still want to leave all of this behind?" It was her last attempt at driving some sense into me.

And just like that, I found myself standing there with my heart in my throat, with the discomfort of leaving one love for another; for having to choose one over the other! The cool air blowing out of the air-conditioner couldn't dissipate the heat of hot tears threatening to spill-over. So instead I hugged her, and hugged everyone around me who were solemnly watching me, not knowing what to say!

Being the last working day, our school's academic advisor was there too. She was the one who had interviewed me for this job many, many years ago. My mentor told her about my resignation and she was shocked. She scolded me lovingly and asked me to take a seat by her side.

I explained and she listened. Though she tried reasoning with me and reprimanded me for throwing away a flourishing career, she also knew in her heart that I had made up my mind. After a brief tête-à-tête, we managed to joke and laugh about some good old times, easing the tension momentarily.

We had our staff lunch together and I bade my good-bye teary-eyed, even though I vowed to come out smiling. Somehow, I knew I was always going to be a part of this big beautiful family! This didn't seem like a final good-bye and that was extremely comforting!

Chapter 17

At home, my experiments with growing plants continued in full fervour. The snake gourds, ladyfinger, *karamani* and tomatoes were growing well. I had been running some experiments and comparing the growth of the plants on my balcony versus the plants growing in sacks on my farm.

While tending to my garden, a thought popped up – how suddenly things have changed; my priorities, my routine and my perspectives. *What am I doing? What made me take this step? Where am I going with this?* I didn't know the answer to any of these! It was scary. The path seemed risky, muddled and so unclear.

As I thought about it for a minute longer, I was startled at what I had gotten into, and more importantly, who I was becoming in the process. From the one who obliged silently to conformity, second-guessed her choices, put everyone before her, would never do anything others didn't approve of, to this new me. Was I the same person?

Ever since this wild thing happened and it's made me a reckless dreamer and had brought out the rebel in me. I realised there were these boxes people put us in. That over time, we started identifying with it so much that we decided to stay in that box. But sometimes destiny had other plans for and if you were lucky, your heart might lead you to something beyond the norms, beyond social constructs and beyond the confines of the known, the expected. It would literally make you face your fears head on and show you what you are capable of.

I had since stopped defining myself as an absolute of something. I didn't want to belong to any box. I realised I was not done growing; I was always in a constant state of becoming, never an absolute of any one thing. Today this was who I was, and tomorrow, who knows. Tomorrow had endless possibilities.

***

The more people expressed shock about my decision, the more I realised that this probably wasn't a path many chose, and therefore it seemed odd or even weird to many. That set me up early on, to *not* expect resonance and validation from others. This was my journey. My unique journey. It may not be for others and that was okay. Not everyone was at the same point in life and it was absolutely okay to be where we were at any given moment.

You couldn't understand the other's journey unless you have travelled their path. Everyone is at a different place in this journey of awareness about various things that concern us; maybe it was the quality of food that we were consuming and the lifestyle we were leading that bothered me. But food is universal, because it is the life-force. *Shouldn't it concern us all?*

Probably that was the reason I was troubled so much? Seeing such passive response to how the food was being handled. Why was there no mass agitation on how our food was treated? Why was there silence on the pesticide menace?

Why were we not holding the food and drug industries accountable for preservative overuse and antibiotic abuse? What were we going to do about the ill-effects of chemical farming, hybrid invasion, systemic destruction of seed diversity and seed monopoly? More importantly, how many of us were even aware of these things?

Maybe that was what disturbed me to an extent that I couldn't continue living passively anymore. I couldn't continue pacifying myself with the phrase 'I am helpless, I can't do anything to change things around me'. These phrases kept me in the victim mode and kept me stuck, and allowed me the privilege to put on my blinders and go on with my life.

I didn't have all the answers, but I also couldn't sit idle waiting for someone to give me the answers.

I also understood that all of this food adulteration/ preservative menace and everything was our own creation. It was targeted towards consumers who were too busy to make time to prepare these at home. Our convenience culture and break-neck speed lifestyle was part of the problem. The culture told us what success looks like, culture dictated our lifestyle choices and we merely fell for it without looking deeper at the issue.

As I try unpacking all of this, I started to understand what I was seeking! I understood how difficult it was to break free of the comfortable moulds that we lived in – 'the supermarket and hypermarket mould', 'the order online mould', 'the shunning small farmers and grocers for comforts of shopping at air-conditioned one-stop-shops mould'.

It was very difficult and almost impossible to break free from these moulds in our super busy lifestyles. I knew because I was part of the same mould. But beyond all these constraints, somewhere it hit me.

I needed to know how and where my food was grown and how long it took to reach my plate. I needed to be connected with the whole process that sustained me every day. It mattered to me. It mattered a lot!

***

I had a chance to attend an inspiring session on conserving energy and alternative energy resources. I met the legend who had revolutionised the way he lived using only solar energy for his daily needs. After attending the session, I wondered what was taking us so long to use this unlimited bountiful source of solar energy, which was abundantly available year-round in a country like ours.

Not only that, it was a cleaner and greener source of energy too, without any emissions and dependency on fossil fuels. My resolve to go solar was reaffirmed and I was determined to have a solar-powered farm, making a mental note to discuss it with my builder and get the logistics sorted.

With the farmhouse work underway, I was itching to get started on the live fencing on my farm. I knew I had to get started on it early as the plants would take time to grow out and provide us with the much-needed thicket cover, doubling up to provide privacy too. The vision of a green cover surrounding the farm was something I dreamt of always. The two plants I zeroed in on were bamboo and bougainvillea.

I got around twenty saplings of bougainvillea and around seventy-five bamboo saplings from a neighbourhood nursery, and that day we finally started planting them around the edges of the wire fence. There was something about bougainvillea that drew me to them... not sure what it was, but I couldn't think of any other plant lining my fence other than these bright pink and pearly white bougainvillea. We planted three bamboos in a row, alternating with a bougainvillea and then continuing with bamboo and so on throughout the periphery of the farm.

This was the major work that happened that day along with a quick supervision of the construction. As we drove back home tired and content, I could already imagine the dense bamboo covering and the colourful boughs of bougainvillea all over the fence.

A long, hot shower and a cup of ginger tea never failed to perk me up even on the most tiring of days. Once home, I was into my reading and researching mode again. While I was reading about seed saving, I chanced upon an article on an ancient practice.

And I wondered how all the new age advancements couldn't hold a candle to our ancient wisdom. All temples in India typically have a *kalasam* (a kalash or dome) at the top of temple towers. This kalasam is mostly made of metal and is one of the prominent symbols in all the temples. Since ancient times, the kalasam has been filled with *navadanya* (nine grains).

This was practiced to ensure that the seeds were available for growing crops and sustaining life in case of any natural calamities. It was believed that the kalasam being the top most structure in the temple, could withstand any destruction and the survivors of the calamity would have the seeds to cultivate and grow crops again for sustenance.

Such was the importance given to seed saving. They were always thinking about the future generations to come and made sure that the source of our food was preserved and protected. It was a practice that once in twelve years, the grains in the temple kalasams were refilled with a new batch of grain during a festival called 'kudamuzhugu vizha'. As per an inscription, the first *kumbabishekam* was done by King Raja Raja Chola of the Chola dynasty.

Our ancestors had been doing it ever since. What an insightful thing to do! This abundant ancient wisdom prevailed way before all the scientific and technological advancements happened; and today, with all the scientific advancements and developments we had made as a human race, here we were at the stage where we have completely lost over ninety-three percent of our heirloom seeds!

How was this advancement? What were we advancing towards... extinction?

One crucial decision I had made early on was to grow more of native and heirloom variety crops and propagate as many varieties of forgotten crops that were at the brink of extinction. Saving seeds and keeping them in circulation was the only way to save them from becoming extinct. I researched more on farmers who saved heirloom seeds in my region and used every opportunity to meet them and purchase seeds from them.

Chapter 18

Our farm, though just forty-five minutes away from the city, felt like a completely rural place, far-far away from the maddening city crowd. We had come to look forward to our Saturdays. It never felt tiring, never once have we felt like sleeping-in after a hectic five-day work week. On the contrary, there was this bubbling enthusiasm and energy as we approached a Saturday.

As always we got up early, packed our things and hit the road. We drove past the city that was stretching out of slumber with streets slowly getting busy with people and small shops getting ready to be opened. We took in the sights of people walking by, jogging or sipping their morning tea in small tea-stalls and poring over newspaper headlines.

As we crossed the famous Murugan Temple and moved past the temple tank area, the path got narrow and congested as the flower market was busy with its fares. The market place came alive with early morning visitors and devotees thronging the temple road. The adjoining bus depot had drivers and conductors chatting over morning tea as passengers moved in and out of the buses parked there.

As we got past the crowded road, and hit the highway, suddenly the road seemed almost empty. Slowly, the scenery around started to change with buildings and settlements giving way to open green meadows stretching out for miles. For the next twenty minutes, all we saw were stretches of open land, interspersed with paddy fields and wild uncultivated areas.

Once we took a turn into the by-lane towards the village leading to our farm, we found ourselves suddenly transported to a different world. We saw kids running around and playing along the muddy lanes, women tending to household chores, the older members of the family sitting outside their houses, with cows and goats grazing on vast patches of greenery. There was an old government school with colourful pictures drawn on the compound walls.

All I could hear were roosters cock-a-doodling and cows mooing at a distance. It was in stark contrast to the fast-paced city life with sounds of vehicles honking and general chaos. Sounds of women chatting with their neighbours floated in over the rickety fence made of dried twigs and palm fronds that outlined each house. I suddenly felt like an intruder trespassing into this peaceful and quiet place.

My mind was calm and my heart felt lighter and at peace. All the plans and 'to-do' lists we came with, all the urgency we brought with us and all the 'go getter' attitude, just seemed to melt away. Suddenly all that mattered was to slow down and soak in the beauty of this calmness, this delicious slowness of life, this heavenly feeling of travelling through life by foot rather than zooming past in our cars. As we took that turn into the village, it felt like we had suddenly entered into a zone of zen, and our car seemed to be moving in slow-motion. I grabbed the opportunity with both hands to linger... gaze... and just be.

***

I was immersed in attending to the trial garden. As I was bent over pulling out weeds, I heard a loud buzzing coming towards my direction. I turned around right on time to duck my head from these huge black carpenter bees swishing past me.

I was slightly disoriented for a bit, but highly intrigued by the powerful bees that were zig-zagging ferociously over marigold flowers that were growing at a distance.

I stopped my weeding and followed the trail of these bees, utterly fascinated by them. I was instantly able to identify them because I had read about these bees while reading about pollinators sometime back. Seeing them up-close made me quite happy.

Contrary to the prevailing misconception, out of all the 20,000 odd bee species in the world, only five were social bees, building hives and making honey. The rest were 'solitary' bees. There was no social hierarchy of 'queen bee' or 'workers bees'. And the carpenter bee was one of the many solitary bees that led solo lives, and foraged and fended for themselves.

I remembered how I got pulled into their world the more I read about them. They had a significant role as pollinators for some open-faced or shallow flowers, and for some they were actually obligate pollinators, meaning they were exclusive pollinators for certain plants like *Passiflora incarnate* and *Orphium* which were not pollinated by any other insects. So, if these bees didn't exist, there would be no passion fruit; the *passiflora* flower would neither get pollinated nor fertilised to become a fruit. It was fascinating to read about these interconnections and webs of inter-dependencies.

I had also read that certain crops like cow pea, legumes like pigeon pea when pollinated by these insects, resulted in having pods that were larger, better shaped, and more nutritious. There was a detailed article on how pollination occurred in certain plants only after they got 'tripped' by these bees. A much complicated, specialised pollination involved these bees, and their role in the survival of certain species of plants had direct correlation.

I continued to follow the bees at a distance, occasionally losing them and then finally finding them on trees, buzzing around the flowers. Knowing that these bee species were the main pollinators of legume crops made me ecstatic that they had found their way to my farm.

I was getting more and more smitten with the bug lives I discovered on my farm. From someone who used to cringe at the sight of creepy crawlies, which by the way I still do sometimes, I was becoming enamoured by their intriguing secret lives.

With a truck-load of work listed out, I sometimes just followed the trail of insects and lost track of the work at hand. I went around admiring the flowers of weeds that were prolifically growing. I would sometimes pull out my phone to capture the pictures of insects with jewel tones that shimmered and sparkled. The beautiful patterns that existed in nature were mesmerising for me, and sometimes they stole away the limited time that I got to tend to my farm.

Mani, I was sure, got annoyed at times at my loitering habit when there was work to be done, but the gentleman he is, he didn't say as much. It was only when I didn't get back to work after a brief wandering that a mild scolding escaped him. I knew he had tried his best to not express it, but one can only have so much patience for a fellow adult who seemed to shun the work and had decided to wander off.

I understood his frustration. I really did. I was annoyed at myself too for not being able to focus on what was important. Well, what *was* important? Wasn't this mindless wandering, following the trail of butterflies important? Wasn't just staring at the beauty of wild flowers important? Wasn't this watching the clouds float around and guessing the birds from their bird calls important? It reminded me of a poem I had read recently:

I meant to do my work today—
But a brown bird sang in the apple-tree.
And a butterfly flitted across the field,
And all the leaves were calling me.

– Richard Le Gallienne

I desperately wished I could compartmentalise and place these activities for leisure time. But it never happened like that. I couldn't make a timetable to slot this under a specific time. A slot that read 'Time for wandering and looking at random things'.

What could I do when these moments came at the most inopportune time? They seemed to always visit me when there was loads of work to be done, what was one to do?

As I walked back, I found a tiny neem tree pushing through mounds of concrete near the driveway. What a place to grow, I wondered. There were hardly any conducive conditions for it to grow. What unthinkable odds it must have overcome in finding a way to sustain. What a great example to show life thrived in all odds and it did not await permission to be lived.

I was foraging again this week. It had become a compulsive activity whenever I was on the farm. The delight of what I would find made me dizzy with excitement. I quietly made my way over the unkempt piece of plot adjacent to the farmhouse area.

"Where are you going?" Mani inquired as I almost reached the spot.

"Nowhere... just here," I replied sheepishly as I waved and smiled.

My eyes shone, wanting to see all that was hidden beneath the shrubbery that was mindlessly stamped. There were leaves shaped perfectly like hearts. There was a purplish red smear right in the centre of the perfect green heart shaped leaf. *What were these*, I wondered. They were so beautiful and exquisite that it almost ached to see them just lying there unnoticed.

One of the ladies from the neighbouring plot came over asking to take some of our coconut shells for firewood and as she passed by seeing me poring over the leaf, she exclaimed loudly that those were *thalikkeerai*, a medicinal green.

My suspicions were confirmed about the vast wisdom hidden in the shrubbery. I clearly instructed my farm helpers to not clear these areas in the jest for weeding out. Because I was not finished investigating this space fully to my heart's content yet.

They laughed out loud and I heard a smirk too as they wondered at my craziness. They surely thought I was a crazy city lady who was over-enthusiastic about everything she found on the farm and got overtly excited over mundane things.

As I walked towards the edge of the plot, I cupped my hands around my mouth and let out a little squeal of joy.

"What have you found this time?"

"Oh, something very amazing..." I almost squealed.

"It's getting late, we need to be packing up so we get back home in time before the kids return from school," Mani was saying loudly.

"Yeah, in a minute," I replied. I watched the beautiful leaves and flowers in various shapes and colours dancing in their little crib. Each one a promise, a possibility of something yet to be discovered. I felt a wave of joy to find these little wonders right on my farm. How lucky was I!

Foraging around our farm grounds and finding interesting herbs and weeds made me a curious and adventurous cook too. I was researching on the new plants that I encountered and feverishly recorded my findings. I learnt how to identify and cook many lesser-known greens that I hadn't been privy to before. It was an interesting time.

Chapter 19

On the farmhouse construction front, things were moving pretty smoothly. The roofing and plastering of walls was almost complete. There was flooring, plumbing, electrical connections still to be done.

Meanwhile, we were focusing on the small outhouse construction to be completed on priority, so we would have a small space to rest and store gardening stuff during our visits. Also, the foundation for the compound wall around the 'soon-to-be' vegetable patch was getting ready too. Once that was through, we could start preparing the land for our vegetables.

That day we had just a few tasks on our list. It involved checking up on the black gram patch and seeing how they were faring. And the next important thing was to check up on our fruit trees. To our utter surprise, the sweet lime, pomegranate and sapota were flowering already. We had purchased these saplings almost 5 ft in height and well matured, so we would get to enjoy the fruits sooner.

As per my notes, plants ready to fruit needed extra potassium and calcium supplement, so we added charcoal ash we had already kept ready the previous week. I also made a mental note to powder my banana peels that I'd kept for drying. They were excellent source of potassium as well.

I had started collecting egg shells too which could be used as calcium supplement. I was turning out to be those ladies drying and powdering various things at home and my kids didn't like it one bit.

As we prepared to leave, Vishal informed that he needed us to pick out the tiles for kitchen and bathroom. We fixed up a time during the week to go tile shopping.

***

It had been raining tiles for nearly two weeks now. We had been tile-hunting along with our builder. Me being extremely picky and choosy, I was pretty sure that by now Vishal was ready to pull-out all his hair! It had been that crazy!

This was our second round of tile shopping. The poor guy hadn't seen this coming. He must've thought he would wrap up the tile selection in one visit. What could I say, I simply didn't like the collection they had at the first store. We met up with Vishal again at this other store he suggested and we started browsing.

Builder: "Browse and let me know if you like something."

Me: "Sure. This one's nice, isn't it? Let's go with this..."

Builder: "Okay ma'am."

(Turns to the salesperson and asks for the design name card and records it for his reference)

Me: (While moving along to look for the next item on the list, I stopped abruptly) "Wait! Look at this one! Isn't this beautiful?"

Builder: "Yes ma'am. (Looking confused now) So finally which one are we going with?"

Me: "The second one for sure."

Our builder, afraid that I might change my mind again, quickly got the details from the salesgirl, and moved briskly towards the elevator to go to the next floor to look at the other items on the list.

Me?... I was still on the same floor looking wide-eyed at all the various options displayed, not quite sure that I had picked the best one and feeling more confused than before. I was walking very slowly while secretly eyeing my third and fourth choices, wondering if it was the best time to announce yet another change! This was pretty much the story of our tile-picking adventure so far. I just prayed that my builder doesn't quit!

***

The period between the months of April to July was proving to be extremely difficult. Difficult because I had been working on my vegetable garden plan for months now, but couldn't implement any ground work yet. The blue print with rows of raised beds was drawn up and ready. I had filled in the vegetables I wanted to grow, marking clear outlines where each one would be planted.

I studied companion planting and factored in a lot of my takeaways into account before I added each crop into a slot. I did an in-depth research on border plants and trap crops that were suitable for my patch. I chose castor, sesbania (*agathi*) and a few papaya trees to plant around the periphery. I chose trap crops carefully to integrate natural pest management practices.

Castor was meant to be an excellent trap crop, and sesbania was greatly useful for increasing biomass for the soil. It also helped as an excellent green manure. Being a leguminous crop, it added nitrogen to the soil, and improved the soil's physical, chemical and biological health. It was proven to promote microbial activity in the soil, maintained nutrient balance and enriched the soil with organic matter, adding a huge biomass.

After reading up about sesbania, I decided to line them up around my vegetable patch. I chose to dot the periphery of my veggie patch with papaya as it was a tree that wouldn't take up a lot of space.

I understood that if I needed to succeed in organic farming, then I had to do things differently. Mono cropping sure had failed the farmers big time and it was definitely not a holistic approach to farming. If I had to manage my crops totally organically, I needed to practice intercropping with a good understanding of companion planting, trap crops and biological pest control methods.

As I poured my time into sketching the plan and researching, my restlessness kept growing. I wanted to see the real garden soon; the one which currently existed on paper and in my dreams. But I had to wait. And wait I did... But in the meantime, I did sufficient research and got things ready to start the moment it was mid-July, the month of *Aadi*, the auspicious sowing season.

As I dug deeper into the soil health arena, I was astounded by this ginormous inter-web of microbial world that existed in the soil. As they say, the more we read, the more we realise how little we really know. I suddenly entered the fascinating, invisible world of microbes. The world of bacteria, fungi and their beautiful network of mycelium supplies water and nutrients to the plants under the ground. The soil is therefore alive and teeming with life! This soil with numerous microbes made our land fertile and is life-giving. But being invisible to human eye, they were disregarded of their very existence.

It was at that moment that my love for an unkempt garden was born. I learnt what disservice we do as humans in creating manicured gardens. In an attempt to have a clean garden, we remove the undergrowth and bushes, wiping out an entire mini ecosystem.

This only resulted in keeping out a number of beautiful birds. Birds found insects in leaf litter. The leaf litter also eventually decomposed and became manure for the plants growing in that space. Plants shed leaves so those leaves can again go back to the soil and become a source of nourishment to the plants. But by sweeping a garden clean, a wonderful food source got completely wiped out.

It made me wonder, how disconnected we have become to everything around us!

***

I checked on my black gram crop and it was almost ready for harvest. I walked over to the far-off corner where our little make-shift trial gardening was going on in some jute bags and picked some tomatoes and chillies that I had planted a couple of months back. This was my practice garden in little bags, and I was deliriously happy to see my first harvest. The brinjals and chillies were ready to be harvested, and the flowers were blooming as well.

Chapter 20

May 2018

With school closed for summer, we made sure to get the kids to the farm the following weekend.

The car ride to the farm was a dream ride, especially if we took the scenic route of East Coast Road, which was a four-lane highway built along the coast of the Bay of Bengal.

When you hit the road early in the morning, the scenic sea route was pretty amazing. A peek to the left revealed a glistening silver strip of the mighty ocean graciously folding its waves along the stretch. The dense casuarina vegetation interspersed with stretches of glistening waves drenched in the morning sun rays, was nothing short of a mesmerising view!

The rising sun in the horizon filled the sky with a deep orange flame, setting the clouds ablaze. The waves rolled along the shore in a rhythmic manner, coming forth and receding as if dancing with the land.

The days when we're just the two of us, we would opt for melodious Ilaiyaraja classics on some days and sometimes preferred driving in silence. Some days were for quiet reverence. The sights and sounds were immersive and we drowned willingly into the depths of this mystic beauty of nature that surrounded us. It commanded our senses to complete surrender. We'd be in a meditative trance!

That day though, it had to be kids' choice of the latest peppy beats that put us all in an upbeat mood. But not for long! No sooner had we settled and reached a harmonious state, the dreaded routine started.

P: "Can we change the song? We have heard this so often.

M: "No, don't! I love that song."

P: "Why does she always get to choose? It's not fair."

M: "No, you are the one who always gets to choose. Today is my turn."

P: "No, I don't."

M: "Yes you do."

P: "No, I don't."

Me: "Okay, quiet now! I am switching off the music. No music for the rest of the drive."

M: "It's not fair, Mummy. Why can't I have what I want?"

M: "Can you turn off the AC? I am feeling cold."

P: "No, Mummy, don't. I am sweating."

M: "Hey, can't you see I am shivering? Please switch it off."

P: "No, don't..."

Me: "Can you guys ever agree on anything?"

M: "Look, Mummy, he is bothering me?"

P: "No, I'm not."

M: "Yes you are."

Me: "Will you both stop it, already?"

Silence for two minutes...

P: "Are we there yet?"

M: "When will we reach? How much longer?"

P: "I am hungry."

M: "And I have to use the restroom."

All this during a forty-five-minute ride. Any road trip was a pain as both the kids hate travelling. As much as we all loved visiting new places, travelling to the destination was the most agonising part for them. They constantly wished there was time-travel possible so they could simply bypass the torture.

This was the one thing that was common among these polar opposites – hate for travel. They were homebodies and were at their happiest when home. After a quick pit stop at our favourite breakfast joint, we continued towards our farm.

The kids seemed to be in a good mood after the scrumptious breakfast. They seemed to have made a pact and came up with some terms and conditions for the rest of the journey ahead.

At the farm, the black gram crop looked glorious and ready for harvest. Though we never expected any harvest from this crop, it surprised us with plenty of pods. With kids around for this activity, the four of us spent a good amount of time harvesting the pods.

Though the only idea of this crop was to enrich the soil with nitrogen, the harvest ended up pretty good. Once we finished harvesting the pods, I instructed my farm help to get the patch tilled so that the plants along with its roots and stem got mixed with the soil. This would be our green manure.

The first step towards soil preparation was done and we were ready for the next. Once tilled, the soil had to be left undisturbed for some time, until we got ready to start our raised beds.

***

The reason I decided on preparing raised beds was because the soil on my farm was predominantly claycy, and had very little organic matter. The land had been barren for many years now and prior to that probably it was part of chemical farming which resulted in the soil being completely lifeless. My plan was to focus primarily on soil fertility and worked extensively on getting the soil ready before the sowing season.

It was already May and we had to get started on our raised beds so the organic matter had enough time to slowly decompose and be ready when the seeds got sown.

Being the first time that we were building raised beds, initially I wanted an expert to guide us with it. So, I had consulted with a few of them and had been waiting for them for months to give me their dates. After constant follow through and long stretches of unresponsiveness, I decided to take it upon myself. I wasn't ready to risk waiting for someone to help me while I let the sowing season pass me by.

I doubled down and read up every piece of information available on building raised beds. I made extensive notes and took bits and pieces of various details and created one that suited my needs. Now all I needed was the confidence that I could do it without any expert guidance.

***

The farmhouse was shaping up beautifully. It was like a dream coming true in front of my eyes! The Santorini inspired colour scheme and the western cottage-style look that I had envisioned had been difficult to explain at first, because down south, a farmhouse typically wore a very traditional look. So to explain this fusion look took some time, but luckily, we had a contractor and builder who were ready to experiment, and made all the effort to replicate that look for me.

As a last-minute addition, I decided on an accented brick wall adjacent to the staircase that went up to the first floor. All through the staircase, I wanted glass fixed at regular intervals to give a 360 degree view of the farm and greenery. In the space below the landing, I dreamt of a space lined with book shelves and a large day bed with cushions piled high for my kids to sprawl across reading books, drenched in the delicious warm sunlight streaming through the window.

The colour scheme for the floor and tiles were all whites, off-whites and neutrals. I also wanted a small veranda running all around the house, supported with white pillars. So far, the construction was coming along on-point.

The pace was good and there were no delays or glitches whatsoever. The work went on according to the dates for hand-over pretty well, and every time I visited the farm there was a major development, and my dream house was gradually becoming a reality.

For homebodies like us who couldn't be bothered with any programs during weekends, we now eagerly waited to visit our farm. Getting up early on weekends was something we hated with a vengeance, but when it was a farm visit, we looked forward to it with excitement. With work moving at a good pace and the farm buzzing with activities, we started going to the farm as early as possible, so we could take care of a couple of things before it got too sunny and hot.

That day's most important agenda was to prepare an exhaustive list of electrical points needed in the farmhouse. We went around every inch of the building, carefully navigating workers busy plastering, drilling and the uneven floor littered with cement sacks and equipment. We pictured ourselves living in this space and thought about the electrical points we might need.

"I would need a plug-point here on this kitchen island. What if I am working on my laptop and I need to charge it?" I said.

"Okay, add that to your list and we can get it done," Mani replied.

"But I want it to be hidden from plain sight. I don't want my beautiful island to look ugly..." I said.

Mani rolled his eyes and started moving ahead saying something in the lines of, "Why don't you figure out the location of the said plug-point and we can tell Vishal? I am sure he will think of something that works."

Well, that was a smooth escape, I'd say.

But this made me realise that this 'listing the electrical point work' was going to take some serious consideration and foresight. A lot of visualisation exercises needed to be done. A thorough study followed, which meant me standing in front of walls for extended periods of time, making gestures and mumbling incomprehensible stuff, startling the wits of the workers and getting weird stares from them.

But that couldn't distract me. I was a woman on a mission. After what seemed like an excruciatingly long time, I got the work done, ran it past Mani and explained it to the electrician.

Chapter 21

The last two days were spent in finalising the plan for the raised garden beds and the blue-print was ready; I had a full chart of drawing complete with colour coding and all the details. We needed three important components for this – bricks to line the boundary of the beds, lots of dried leaves/ sugarcane bagasse for organic matter and aged cow dung manure. We had ordered a tractor load of cow dung manure from the neighbouring village and it was deposited near the designated area. We got the regular bricks through our building contractor.

All we needed now was the organic matter. After enquiring around for dried plant matter in and around the village, we realised that we might not be able to procure enough of those. That was when the idea to approach sugarcane juice vendors in the city hit us. Having never approached strangers to part with their waste before, it was quite difficult, not to mention embarrassing at first.

But all we needed to do was ask and found that the juice vendors were more than happy to give us the waste husks post juicing. They were in fact, delighted that we were making their lives easier by taking the waste off of their hands. One man's waste was another man's treasure, indeed!

For the ground work, we first had to measure out and mark the number of beds we were planning. After careful observation and measurement, we decided on seven raised beds, each 40 ft in length and 4 ft wide. We left a gap of 2 ft between beds to accommodate walking space. We then lined the measured beds with bricks to contain the layers intact.

We hired extra farm helpers for this project and explained the whole process step-by-step to them.

Once the skeletal structure was ready, we started layering the beds with three components:

First, a layer of dried sugarcane waste (for organic matter, we also added dried leaves and grass to the mix; this became food for the earthworms and for the essential microbes in the soil)

Then a layer of cow dung manure (for adding nutrition to the soil)

Then a layer of our garden soil.

Repeat twice again with a layer of dried sugarcane bagasse, a layer of cow dung manure, and finally a layer of garden soil to finish the beds.

Three such consecutive layering had to be done across the length and breadth of each bed.

So far in two days, four such beds were made ready and there were three more to go. It became amply clear that I had to travel during the weekdays alone to get the raised beds done. We couldn't leave the work mid-way and wait for the weekend to finish it. With Mani having to go to work, I decided to get an acting driver to drive me up and down for the next three days of work.

On Monday morning, I took along some fruits for breakfast and packed my lunch and started for the farm. On the way, I called Velu to ensure that the workers were coming for work. Once at the farm, work started right on the dot.

The workers by now were familiar with the rigmarole of layering the raised beds, so after the initial rounds of working alongside them, I found a spot under the coconut palm to rest a bit. There were two palm trees right in the middle of the patch casting shade partially on the first and second raised beds.

I made a note of this and realised that I might have to make corrections in my blue print and interchange the crops that I had initially planned for this space. With minimal sunlight on these beds, it was ideal to plant greens and herbs. Sun loving crops might not thrive here. As I got up to inspect the work, my phone rang.

"*Hello, Eppadi ma iruke*?" Dad's voice chimed in.

"*Appa*, I am good, how are you? Hope you are regular with your morning walks?" I enquired.

"Yes, *ma*. I don't miss a day," he said proudly.

"How's the terrace garden coming along, pa?" I asked about his favourite hobby. He had a green thumb and grew plenty of greens and vegetables in the terrace in grow bags.

"The brinjals and lady fingers are fruiting in plentiful and we had a good harvest of tomatoes too. Only the gourds aren't coming up well due to the heat," he sounded distracted as I could hear mom pestering him to hand over the phone to her.

"Here, talk to your mom."

"*Amma, pesaren ma*," mom said in her sing-song-y voice. The excitement in her voice was evident and I could almost visualise her eyes twinkling.

"Amma, how are you? What's cooking for lunch?" I asked while instructing the workers on the field with sign language.

"*Yennaikathirikkavathakuzhambu, vendakka poriyal, thakkalirasam* and *appalam*," she listed out excitedly.

"Hmm, so basically you guys are enjoying 'garden to table' food," I teased her.

"Yes, yes, of course!" she said sounding pleased.

"And what did you make for lunch and what's that sound? Are you out somewhere?" she inquired.

"Yes, Amma. I am at the farm today," I said.

"But it's Monday. Is *mappilai* (aka Mani) there along with you?" I already knew how this conversation was going to proceed henceforth.

"Mmm... no, he isn't. It's a working day for him. He had to go to office today," I replied knowing very well the long lecture that was going to ensue.

"Please don't travel alone this far. How many times have I told you?" And she rattled out the same dialogue I had heard umpteen times.

"Amma, we have the raised beds work going on here and it has to be supervised till it's completed. I can't just leave it to the farm workers. They don't know how to go about this. Plus, I am here with our regular trustworthy call driver, Ramalingam," I added, hoping this would put her frazzled nerves to rest.

"But get back home early, before it gets dark, okay?" she sounded upset.

"Yes, ma. I'll be starting back post lunch. So, stop worrying now," I almost scolded her.

"*Seri, seri*. Call me when you get home," she said as we hung up.

The raised beds weren't exactly a weekend project and therefore I had to go to the farm every day till all the beds got done. Packing my lunch and leaving in the morning with the sun at its scorching best, it had been a hell of a hectic few days. But it was so fulfilling to finally see the garden beds that existed only as a sketch in my notebook and in my dreams up until now.

As we progressed with the raised beds every day, I could see my paper sketch come alive. It was quite an exhilarating feeling. To see something that you only saw in your mind's eye and then to put it on paper and finally getting to see it in reality was an amazing feeling.

This was the first and the most comprehensive work we got done towards our organic vegetable gardening project. Suddenly, the farm project didn't seem so elusive anymore. I could actually feel it all falling into place.

A major piece of the puzzle was set in motion and I could see the big picture. I felt a wave of accomplishment wash over me as I stood at a distance and saw all the seven beds neatly done. Things started to look promising. It wasn't just going to remain a dream anymore... it wouldn't be long now!

***

Between all this work, I wandered off admiring the beautiful weeds growing on my farm. There were some herbs and weeds I had not seen since my childhood years. And one such was *Thumbai poo*. Ever since I noticed these, I started yearning for a herb garden, maybe a tiny little corner dedicated for these precious herbs.

And one day I somehow convinced Mani that we really did need a little herb garden on our farm. I made a list of native herbs in my notebook and during my very next visit to our local nursery, picked up all kinds of herbs I could find there. I had this idea of creating a mini rock garden of sorts to house these medicinal herbs and precious 'weeds' there.

I didn't dare discuss the rock garden idea with Mani. I decided to slip it in as we started the planting process and deal with his reaction then. For now, I focused on researching on each of those herbs and their medicinal benefits and compiled them neatly in a folder on my computer.

Finally, it was the day we were to plant thse herbs. We had some extra farm workers to help us in some other chores on the farm, and I casually mentioned my idea of the rock garden, and got some of the helpers to move some of the rocks lying around on the property to the spots I had identified for them. I had to say that the project went on quite smoothly and Mani took it surprisingly well too. In fact, he loved the idea and the final look of it.

We now had around fifteen to twenty herbs that included *kesavardini, vetrilai, karisilangani, thooduvalai, maasipacchai, nilavembu, mint, tulasi, nocchi, chitharathai, mudakathan, poonaimeesai, thippili, agragar, lemongrass, karuveppilai, thumbai poo* and *keezhaneli.*

I was hoping to keep adding more to the family soon. I was exploring ways to use each one of those and learn more about their traditional usage. While I stuck to the traditional recipes with some, I loved experimenting and finding new ways to use all that grew on my farm. I first made *kesavardhini* hair oil for M. Next was a delicious salad I concocted – the *Thumbai poo* salad!

As I worked on putting together this particular recipe, I was taken back to the times I had first encountered it. My earliest memory of this flower was during the quintessential Sunday oil baths of my childhood days. The ritual of an oil bath was kind of legendary in the southern regions of India and was practiced religiously.

Sesame oil was heated and a few grains of raw rice added, and once it crackled, some of these white *thumbai poo* flowers would be added as the oil was removed from fire. This lukewarm oil would be generously applied on our heads and massaged into our scalps, dripping all over our face. It had to soak through for at least an hour before we were allowed to wash it off. We followed it, disgruntled, knowing better not to question these practices back then. Now I sat there nodding in approval of it as I read the benefits. It seemed to have tons of medicinal properties. Age and experience had taught me that some things were always understood better in hindsight. Better late than never, like they say!

This salad is as close to a 'farm-to-table' recipe as it gets:

Recipe:

Radish greens—½ cup

Raw papaya—½ cup

Red Radish—¼ cup

Pasalaikeerai—½cup

Thumbai poo—a handful

Salad dressing: I made a simple vinaigrette using lemon juice, olive oil, crushed garlic, salt and pepper powder. The result was amazing.

And to think that salads were mainly associated with cucumber, lettuce and carrots... well, a few misconceptions were cleared today. To top it off, I was bowled over by the fresh burst of flavour from the vegetables from my trial garden and flcwers foraged from my farm. With every morsel, the freshness and flavours exploded, taking my taste buds to an exotic adventure.

It was so delicious and refreshing! My outlook about salads completely flipped 360 degrees as I started exploring the weeds and greens growing on my farm.

Chapter 22

A week after harvesting the black gram, I turned my attention to de-seeding the black gram pods. They had been drying in my balcony all this while. This was the first time I was doing it. The activity was beyond my wildest imagination for sure.

Good lord! What was happening here! I was so smitten by the black gram I laboured over for days to de-seed that I decided to use the whole urad without removing the skin in my idli batter.

Though the batter wasn't exactly white and my idlis didn't turn out as pristine white as *mallipu* (a saying in Tamil, meaning as white as jasmine flowers), I was ecstatic. Except for the colour, there was no change in taste or texture of the idli, and what was more, the outer skin on the lentils added fibre to the dish.

If anyone would've had any problems with the colour of the idlis that day, they would have faced my wrath, because man, was I ready to put up a fight! Now I know why farmers come off a wee-bit crazy sometimes. Only those who grew food themselves understood and appreciated the full range of emotions that came with it.

***

The next huge task at hand was to get my seeds sorted for sowing. The auspicious month of Aadi was just two weeks away. I got ready to sort through my seeds and started prepping. I had sourced seeds from an heirloom seed-saver I had come to know, and had procured all the varieties I wanted to grow.

I was so overcome with excitement that I didn't know where to start for a while. I kept going back and forth about whether I should start with a few seeds now and then the others later, or go ahead with all of them at once. Finally, after wasting a considerable amount of time in an analysis-paralysis state, I decided to go all in. Yeah, what the heck! I was going to plant every single one of them suitable for the season.

I charted out a plan to segregate the seeds that needed direct sowing and the ones which could benefit from soaking in water for a few hours. Now, as always, I had read up on all and sundry about seeds and sowing, and there was quite a lot of information available on which seeds could be sown directly and which ones need transplanting. Though I had read up as much as I possibly could on the subject, I decided to do what made sense to me... if it worked out then all was well and if it didn't, then I'd learn something new.

So the first step was soaking the seeds. Soaking the seeds before planting them was a sure shot way to jump start and speed up the germination process. But I was careful not to soak the tinier ones, especially the greens, as it was easier to scatter them on some good soil when dry.

The ideal soaking duration was eight to twelve hours. I had soaked my seeds in the morning and I was planning to sow them in the evening. I didn't have enough seed trays at this point, and while I was looking for containers to start my seeds in, I came across a stack of *dhonnai* (bowls shaped out of dried *mantharai* leaves used for distributing *prasadam* in temples) that we had purchased long back for some family event.

After much contemplation, I decided to start my seeds in those small dhonnai. I felt it would make it easier during transplanting as I could just place them directly in the soil and wouldn't have to worry about disturbing the roots in the process. These one-leaf-thick dhonnai could be placed in the soil directly as they were biodegradable and would slowly decompose in the soil.

While the seeds were soaking, I filled each of the seed trays and dhonnai with potting mix and kept them ready. These containers covered the entire length and breadth of my living room floor. I asked the kids to stay off the area. I said it a bit sternly for good measure because I couldn't afford to have any nuisance around them.

Once the seeds were done soaking, I carried on with the tedious process of sowing all the seeds carefully. Tucking in each teeny tiny seed into the dark depths of the potting mix with my heart filled to the brim with hope of what was to come. With each seed, I sent a prayer up. Only I knew the intensity of this moment and how momentous of an occasion this was for me!

With paralysing trepidations on one side and immense faith on the other, I carried on with the task. I realised in that moment, the collective hope of farmers all over who plant seeds over and over and over again, every season.

Once the sowing was done, I proceeded to water the containers and carefully placed the tags with the names of each plant. I then moved the containers into my store room and covered them with newspapers. The reason to keep them covered in a dark room was that firstly, seeds didn't need sunlight for germination. They only needed moisture and warmth. Secondly, covering minimised evaporation of water and kept the seeds moist longer and also trapped heat to provide warmth.

Now came the difficult part. Each day I would check on them, water them and see if they had sprouted. Nothing had taught me patience quite like waiting on my seeds to sprout. Every day I threw longing glances at them, hoping I'd catch them right when they were pushing through the soil and popping out. Alas, I had to be patient.

So for the time being, I had to distract myself so I didn't end up checking upon them too often and disturb them in the process. I went back to reading *The One Straw Revolution* by Masanobu Fukuoka that had been holding my attention quite well during these times.

Fast rather than slow, more rather than less — this flashy 'development' is linked directly to society's impending collapse. It has only served to separate man from nature, the author writes. In between checking on my seeds, I was voraciously devouring this book that was keeping me from spiralling down the 'what if nothing germinates?' negative thought loop.

Thankfully, some of the seeds started sprouting by the third day and I jumped with glee. My heart skipped a beat as I ran out to announce this to Mani. My faith was restored! So I was not an utter failure. There was hope, what a relief! Mani came in and we both watched the seedlings with wonder, as if we were the first ones to grow something from a seed in all of creation.

Some seeds took up to two weeks to germinate, but almost ninety percent of the seeds sprouted. I was on cloud nine! Every single time I saw a little seedling sprout in one of the containers, pushing through with a crown of soil on its head, standing proudly and soaking up the sunshine, I was ecstatic.

It was like witnessing a miracle. To be able to see the seeds sprouting was the reassurance I so badly needed at that point.

It took a while to realise that this was happening and that it was possible for me to grow things, and that maybe, just maybe, I might realise my vegetable garden dream after all.

It was as if I was sure nothing would sprout. This self-doubt had stealthily crept in when I was going ahead with everything. Then suddenly I got this dreadful feeling that the crucial part wouldn't work. I guess I was expecting some epic fail like that. But I realised then that when you fully trusted the process and took a leap of faith, things worked out. That was just how it was!

Chapter 23

July 2018

Going to the farm on Saturdays had become a sort of a ritual for us. The kids didn't want to be dragged along early in the morning and wanted to sleep in. We were given very stern instructions that they were not to be bothered in the morning.

No amount of cajoling worked and being a very important day on the farm, we didn't put up a fight with them. Not on that day! It was extra special. It was the first day of *Aadi* – the sowing month!

We started bright and early after a hot cup of coffee and wanted to hit the road as early as possible. There were lots of plans for that day. The seedlings were all ready for transplanting and I was excited and tensed at the same time.

Tensed because I was wondering how on earth would we transport all the fifty odd seedlings to the farm without causing them any distress. I picked up a couple of picnic baskets and wide trays and start arranging them neatly. We had to make a dozen trips to the car park before we could load all the plants into the car. I also had a stash of seeds I needed to take for direct sowing.

I was taking the blue-print I prepared for planting in my raised beds. I had marked everything from which vegetable to plant and what border crops to have between them, to even the plants that needed to go in the periphery of the vegetable patch. Everything was colour-coded and very detailed and drawn up to the tee.

I pulled out my trustworthy brown diary, which held all the important dates, details and events regarding the farm, and opened the page to find my to-do list for the day. I made a mental note to remind my caretaker to get more farm helpers today. We would be needing them! I said a quick prayer before starting.

It was a huge day for us. All my efforts, from preparing the soil to sowing and transplanting would be put to test now. Would my efforts work? Would the plants grow?

We got into the car, our minds pre-occupied with a lot of things. Mani was still figuring out how to utilise the space best to accommodate everything that we were lugging around. We had lots to accomplish that day. It was 6:00 a.m. and we'd be reaching the farm around 7:00. I wanted to stop over at a grocer's to buy some chilled soft-drinks for the farm-helpers, but it was too early and there were no shops open yet.

I made a note to self that I needed to plan and buy things the previous day. We treaded along, silently soaking in the early morning quietness. The streets were barren with very minimal activities. The city was slowly waking up from slumber. There were very few people on the streets walking by and a few joggers running along the sidewalks with headphones in place.

Mani drove on silently while I looked out the window with a quiet blissful smile on my face because today was the day – the day we had been waiting for don't know how long, it seemed like forever. And slowly, as we crossed the city limits, he asked me the plan for the day and I listed it out. He nodded and reminded me to call the caretaker before we reached the farm. I nodded and we fell silent again.

Yes, there were days when we were chattering away non-stop. It was mostly about the farm, kids and life. Okay, to be honest, it was mostly me talking. Some days, it was about a disturbing headline of the week which put us both in a solemn and agitated mood where we kept talking and pondering over where the world is heading to and such.

But not that day. That day we were somehow very quiet, the happy quiet. There was this wonderful companionable silence. The content feeling of not needing to fill the silence with words; to be comfortable not talking yet feeling connected; the quiet knowing of what was going on in the other's mind. We sure had a lot on our minds.

Upon reaching the farm, we got to the tasks one by one. There was no time to waste. We rolled through the day with one thing after another with clarity and purpose. We left the weeding and manuring the tree saplings to the extra farm help we had hired for the day and took care of the sowing, transplanting and labelling ourselves.

I kept my brown diary handy and kept drawing columns and wrote down what I had sowed and transplanted in each of the seven raised beds. Though I was going exactly by the blue-print, I had to make some last-minute changes as I noticed some patches getting more sunlight than the others. I had to re-adjust and change the planting plan according to the shade-loving and sun-loving plants.

Because of this, I had to record the changes meticulously, lest we forget what and where we sowed something. The date and the name of the plant had been clearly written and stuck in each of the patches.

Though the farm helpers took their mid-morning break, we continued working till lunch time. We sowed seeds of pumpkin, cucumber, snake gourd, bottle gourd, bitter gourd, radish, long beans, spinach, and six other varieties of greens. We transplanted three varieties of tomatoes, two varieties of chillies too, the long one and the round one, five varieties of brinjal (the long green, the small purple, the striped green and white, the Vellore thorny variety and the purple long).

We planted ridge gourd, cluster beans, French beans, marigold, tulsi, basil and curry leaf saplings. We also planted castor and sesbania on the periphery of the vegetable patch for pest control and biomass.

In one of the shaded patches, I audaciously planted beets, broccoli, capsicum, onion and lettuce. Mani was giving me 'the look' like 'Are you out of your mind? Lettuce in Chennai... really?' But I pretended not to notice him and went about my planting with an air of conviction.

I was secretly praying that at least a few of them grew, just to save my face, though I knew these weren't the crops that could survive the Chennai heat. But one could always hope! And I had lots of it at that point.

***

I was still pinching myself if all this was really happening. Had I just sowed all of those seeds on my farm? Was I living my dream?

For the longest time, I had my doubts about it. With the kids' school and hectic demands on our time, how would this ever be possible? There was a reason why I had always considered this my retirement project. But pretty soon the urge to grow my own food took hold of me.

I wanted to feed organic vegetables and fruits to my growing children! I wanted good, clean food for my family now, not when I was old and my kids were out of the house. I wanted to give my kids exposure to a meaningful co-existence with nature.

In the fast-paced, rat race of the glitzy, noisy world that they were growing up in, I wanted them to have a reference point for a better, more grounded perspective on what was important in life. I wanted them to know that they could follow their own passion and dreams too, no matter how different they looked from others.

I wanted them to have the courage to walk a less-travelled path if that was what their hearts desired. I wanted them to know they didn't have to blindly follow the herd; that they had a choice; that they could pave their own path. And for that I had to walk the talk.

I had to follow my dreams. Our parenting philosophy largely enabled us to work on our dreams and our farm. We believed that our lives did not revolve only around our children.

In today's hyper-parenting climate, this might not be a popular opinion. But in my experience I had found that single-minded obsession over our children was actually detrimental to their growth. When a child has an adult fussing over them constantly, it not only rears poor attitude, insecurity, constant need for validation, but also possible resentment over time. Nothing good ever comes out of overdoing things.

I personally know that it was easy for parents to make everything in life about their child's dreams, goals, and activities. I knew this because I *had been* that parent not so long ago, especially during early motherhood. I was fed on a heavy dose of narrative surrounding sacrificial martyrdom in the name of mothering.

But thankfully I realised soon that it wasn't in the best interest, neither for my kids nor me. As parents, Mani and I had made all of our choices and decisions keeping our children foremost and central. However, we had also maintained the idea that we had our own individual dreams and our own purpose in life too, beyond the title of being parents.

We made sure our children had the best resources, our undivided attention, and time. At the same time, we ensured that we nurtured our own interests too. I saw that this outlook had a positive impact on our kids. As they grew up seeing their parents pursue their interests, it made them strive to live their best lives too.

My favourite lines from Khalil Gibran's poem:

Your children are not your children
They are the sons and daughters of life's longing for itself
They come through you but not from you
And though they are with you yet they belong not to you.
You may give them your love but not your thoughts
For they have their own thoughts
You may house their bodies but not their souls
For their souls dwell in the house of tomorrow.

Chapter 24

August 2018

The days were a blur. I had no idea how the week rushed by and it was soon time to visit the farm, and then the weekends flew past too. Every week we watched the seedlings sprout in awe. With time, the labels faded and we ended up wondering what the saplings were. It was fun to guess and to watch and learn from the different shapes of their leaves.

We would meticulously walk every inch of the space and check the growth of the seedlings. The first week after sowing was the most exhilarating experience, to see most of the seedlings coming up from the ground, reassuring me the soil preparation had been up to the mark. It was like watching a dream come to fruition. Every week, we were noting down the growth and I was recording every little detail in my brown diary.

At home I realised that my manual scribblings were good enough, but I wanted to have a more detailed record of the vegetable patch. I sat with Mani and discussed my requirements and we created excel sheets with all the information. Columns with date of sowing, date of flowering, pest issue, date of fruiting and date of harvest, plus a column for remarks.

My day's routine had drastically changed over the course of starting my farming journey. On any given day, there was a truck load of work to be done, not to mention the mental load of planning things to the last detail. I was constantly amazed at how much I was getting done, and yet I was always in a state of bliss.

The day started early for me and zoomed by until I dropped dead on the bed at the end of the day, completely exhausted, yet with a smile on my face and dreams of a glorious tomorrow in my eyes.

As the farmhouse construction progressed, I made a mental note to talk to the solar panel vendors. I needed them to have a look at our place and give us a quotation. I also had this idea of a pergola at the entrance which would be covered with bougainvillea in time forming a canopy of pink and whites and all the colours.

I loved bougainvillea, and every time I spotted one, I yearned to have them on my farm. We finally managed to find a local metal workshop where we shared our pergola design and got it finalised.

I still had to give the vendor a call and get him to come to the farm the following week for measurements and to start the civil work needed. Lots of things on the list for that week's farm visit.

Though a to-do list worked wonders to keep us on track, through our experience we learnt pretty soon to expect the unexpected. A lot of unexpected things cropped up once we reached the farm and it threw us off all our well-laid plans.

Like that day, we spotted our previous batch of tomato plants all grown up and bending over without much support and needed our immediate attention. The snake-gourd and bitter-gourds had grown so wildly that they needed a trellis to guide them up properly. And I was left wondering... I didn't remember seeing these plants this big; they were just tiny little things the previous week.

So, to hell with the to-do list. We needed to take care of that first! But, we didn't know how to. I would've read-up and watched some YouTube videos if I knew I would need the information, but now it was too late. We had to get going right away. We just had to learn on the job, like we had many times before. Nothing deterred us anymore.

And so, after three hours of building the trellis for tomatoes and gourds under the scorching hot sun, we slumped down under the shade of a neighbouring coconut palm. The wind blew over our sweaty faces and it felt heavenly. After a few minutes of resting, I pulled out my brown diary to check my to-do list and found that we hardly ticked off anything in that. It was already too late by then, but I was glad we tackled what needed to be done.

The pergola guy arrived at that moment and we got up to show him the place and go over the details. Meanwhile, the solar vendor too walked in and we finally managed to get a quote and understand all the logistics behind going the solar way and fixing the net-meter with the electricity board.

By the time we were done with them, it was time for us to leave. We had to be back home before the kids got home from school. So we gave a few instructions to our caretaker and knew it in our heart that only a few would happen, but still rattled off the list for our own satisfaction and headed towards the car.

We never seemed to get enough time on the farm, ever. As always, I dreamt of a time when we could live on the farm someday and be able to tick-off everything on our lists.

The journey back to the city started with a lot more planning for the forthcoming week, and to catch up on the ones pending from that day's list. After I fervently jotted down the things Mani rattled off and added a few of my own, I finally closed the diary to lay back on the seat and closed my eyes. We rolled the windows down for the breeze to dry our sweat-drenched faces.

Bone tired and deliriously happy – was this combination ever possible? I guess it was!

***

The week whooshed by. On Saturday, it was raining incessantly. We left the house early, thinking it would stop soon and made a big list of things to do. I got to visit my farm only once or twice a week and I had to travel for roughly an hour to reach there, so I didn't think rain could be an excuse not to take care of things I had already planned.

Throughout the day, the rain didn't stop even for a minute. Though it wasn't pouring, there was this continuous drizzle all through the day. So we worked, sometimes with an umbrella, and sometimes with an oversized hat or just a towel wrapped around our heads.

We transplanted the tomato seedlings, did a lot of weeding, arranged the bricks bordering the raised bed that had fallen off in the previous day's rain, added my kitchen waste to the compost pit, harvested some greens, sowed many more seeds in two more beds and name tagged each patch.

We had started composting in a bigger way now that we had more space to add our kitchen waste. Because it was given that organic gardening and composting went hand in hand, the 'black gold' was definitely a faithful companion for any organic farmer. I had read a lot about different methods of composting and each one seemed a bit more complicated than the previous one.

If a lay person wanted to understand about composting, this information overload seemed enough to discourage anyone.

Composting was basically allowing the organic matter to decompose efficiently to be used as a highly nutritious manure for plants. At home, I followed a very systematic composting procedure. But at the farm with a lot of things that needed my time and attention, I didn't want composting to be complicated.

So here was what I did:

1. *Dug multiple pits in the far corners of my farm and some in the centre.*
2. *Started dumping kitchen waste (veg scraps, fruit peels, etc), garden waste (dried leaves, twigs, grass cuttings) and cow dung. I tried to layer wet waste and dry waste alternatively to maintain the moisture level.*
3. *Sprinkled enough garden soil to cover the waste.*
4. *Repeated step 2 then step 3, and kept repeating the process till the pit was full.*
5. *Sprinkled a little water to keep the pile moist, aiding the microbes to work their magic.*
6. *Gently stirred the pile periodically to aerate.*

That was it. Basically dumped, sprinkled soil and repeated. All my kitchen waste turned into this wonderfully nutritious manure for my plants. I was sure this would make any organised meticulous composter shudder, but this worked for me and that was enough.

Like any other aspect of organic gardening, I read a lot about composting too. The wet (green) matter is basically the nitrogen component and the dry (brown matter) is the carbon component of the compost. Both in the right proportion got composted into a beautiful black manure that was absolutely wonderful for the plants' growth. Why waste the precious kitchen scraps when they could add to the soil's health without spending any money. Plus, it was all organic!

Aside this, what awaited us after three days of glorious showers were weeds! Luxuriantly growing weeds. So along with our existing plans to review the farmhouse work, weeding got added to the list. There were things we planned and there were things we ended up doing. This had become a reality for us and we had made peace with it.

You toiled and made your garden beds with all the wonderful things your seeds would love and what do you see – weeds. No one invited them, but they were the ones happily gorging on all that food carefully laid out for my select plants. So weeding was the major work, apart from other farm related stuff we took care of that day.

We also managed to take care of some business related to the house-warming ceremony for our farmhouse. The construction was almost complete. So when it came to picking an auspicious day for the ceremony, we picked an earlier date so we could start living there sooner.

Another very important task accomplished the previous day, apart from weeding, was building the rest of the trellises for all the climbers. Now that the climbers had started growing, their lateral shoots and tendrils had started looking for support. We had to act quickly and build a trellis to support their growth.

We had been making trellises using old twigs, palm tree fronds and coir ropes. We had to start looking at permanent trellis solutions soon.

Chapter 25

August 2018

There was a lot of planning needed to be done for the following week. The house-warming ceremony date got finalised and we were suddenly in celebration mode. I couldn't believe that the farmhouse construction was almost nearing completion!

In the last eight months or so, we had a tunnel vision of what lay ahead; we rode the days with passion and were so immersed in doing all the things we did, that it was hard to see how these past months rolled by.

We had laboured hard over our dear farm for these months. We had prepared raised beds from scratch, built the fencing around the farm, prepared nurseries, built trellises, sowed, weeded and showered our love upon every little seed, weed, bug and flower here on the farm. And after all these months, the fruits of our labour had not been realised yet.

For the world, it might look like a fool-hardy thing to do – pouring our hard-earned money, time, effort and energy into something that hadn't yielded anything. But we knew what it had provided us – a heart full of joy, promise and a great source for finding our bliss.

This following week was going to be a roller-coaster ride for sure. I was already panicking. As much as I loved celebrating this moment, I was also not someone who was comfortable with any ritualist ceremony. It may be because I had only been witnessing ceremonies where rituals invariably caused tension among people and left a bitter after taste.

The emphasis on rituals became far more important than focussing on the blessed event.

There were tons of protocols on what was to be done, who was to do it, how it was supposed to be done and in which particular order it had to happen. All this made me jittery. Even with careful execution, invariably something would go off, someone would get offended and the whole premise of celebrating someone's blessed event would turn ugly. Not to mention some major cracks in relationships would seep in too. What good were these rituals then, I wondered.

Both Mani and I weren't people who were particular about rituals. We deeply cared about people and did things that made sense to us, but following a ritual mindlessly wasn't for us. Following through with a set of rituals in a particular sequence and making sure nothing was amiss was an added pressure that made me uncomfortable. Walking on eggshells wasn't something I look forward to.

Ceremonies were high tension zones where formalities preceded everything else. That was why I preferred celebrations where there were no formalities or rituals to follow; celebrations where I only needed to focus on sharing my happiness with my loved ones, nothing more! Rituals that brought in rifts weren't even worth having around and that was my opinion. But I guess, to each their own.

We booked a priest for the occasion, bought pooja items as per the list given by the priest, bought gifts for the relatives, discussed the menu and booked a caterer for meals to be served, booked rental furniture and lights and all and sundry that went along with preparing for a house-warming ceremony. There were a gazillion things to be checked off.

In all of this, I also wanted the event to be a bit classy, so I bought some colourful table cloths to be spread over the tables for the guests. Mani being extra cautious of the smoke that filled the room during the yagna/havan, made sure the priest chose a shorter version of the shloka chants to wind up the ceremony sooner to avoid people getting teary-eyed and smoke filling up their lungs. I concurred that it was indeed a thoughtful idea.

Well, as always, good intentions weren't appreciated. No matter what, your best intentions would be misread and made into the worst-case scenario. The celebration inevitably ended with some unexpected drama.

But of course, was it even qualified as a ceremony in Indian households if there wasn't high-tension drama involved? I guess we passed the test with flying colours then! Well, all the highs we were experiencing with our farm had to be balanced out with some lows, I guess.

The ceremony was over. The guests left, rental equipment returned and the celebratory lights came down. We were back to our routine. We focused on the realisation of how blessed we were to have created a haven for ourselves. Only we knew what it had taken to create something brick by brick.

***

It was Saturday already! I don't know when Saturday had become my favourite day. I prepped the day before with my 'things to do on the farm' list and I felt much more in control. I thought I'd be able to crack the unattainable target of 'ticking all the things on my to-do list' this time around.

That day, the kids had school and so we got up early and packed our lunches along with theirs and got ready with the kids, so we could utilise every minute we got. We had to get back before the kids got home, which was around four p.m.

We waved goodbye to the kids, locked up the house and were on our way to the farm. I checked the umpteen number of bags that I was carrying to make sure I had taken everything I needed. Oh, in case you were wondering what these umpteen number of bags contained – well, there was one with our breakfast and lunch of course, and then one with all the seeds we needed to sow to be taken to sow and one with extra clothes, caps, sunglasses and loads of towels; because we invariably changed at least two set of clothes as we got drenched in sweat (yeah gross, but true).

The towels doubled up as something to cover our heads with when it got too sunny and to also wipe the sweat off our faces, to clean our muddy hands and other numerous usages of course. Among other things, we always carried the compost bin to the farm every week to transfer the kitchen scarps I collected at home. And of course, there was another bag with little tools and instruments that the husband needed to fix the new tap fixture.

Oh! And also some neem oil, turmeric and garlic for preparing the natural pest control solution. Because yes, finally we were ready for some face-off with pests!

So, there. That was what were in the numerous bags that we carried every week.

As we started moving, I pulled out my brown diary to rattle out the day's to-do list. The vegetable garden had been thriving well, and now I started getting a little restless about growing the other things I always wanted to grow.

There were ginger, garlic and turmeric I would like to grow on my farm. And I also wanted to grow all the pulses that we consume – toor dal (pigeon pea), moong dal (green gram), urad dal (black gram) and channa dal (chick pea). I had already grown black gram as a nitrogen fixing crop and that gave me the confidence that I could grow pulses too. So that day's to-do list went like this:

Plant ginger and garlic.
Sow seeds for lettuce and broccoli.
Clear out the old cucumber patch.
Plant the second batch of cucumber seeds.
Plant second batch of bitter gourd seeds.
A new flower patch around one of the coconut trees.
Clear out a new patch for pumpkin in the front yard.
Clear an area for cantaloupe.
Prepare the side yard for making trellis for gourds.
Prepare turmeric and garlic solution to spray on plants.
Prepare neem emulsion for pest control.
Harvest lemon grass, palak and curry leaves.

Mani frowned at the impossible list of things, but didn't say anything to me about it. This exhaustive list seemed like a far-fetched dream to accomplish, but we were used to over-planning by now. Whether we were able to accomplish the tasks or not was secondary; making a list with all that our heart aspired to get done was primary.

Chapter 26

A few more saplings were welcomed into the farm two weeks ago. Two banana varieties; *rasthali* and *ellaki*; two papaya saplings, a guava, a gooseberry and a neem sapling. Also, my Singapore Cherry plant had lots of flowers now and I could already spot a few cherries here and there. It was wonderful to see butterflies and sunbirds fluttering around it.

The weekend that followed was the first that I missed going to the farm. The kids' annual day at school was on Saturday, and I had been personally invited to attend the event. Mani was out of town on work too and so the week's farm visit had to be skipped.

I had a great time meeting my ex-colleagues (it feels weird to add the prefix 'ex', but that was the reality). There was a lot of squealing when my friends saw me walk into the auditorium; there were hugs galore and lot of affectionate exchanges that made my heart swoon.

It was such a different experience to be a guest at the school function where I had been a host for nine long years. For once, I sat back and enjoyed the show without having to cater to students backstage and manage the show with my colleagues.

***

To make it up for the last weekend, we went to the farm on a weekday the following week. And what did we see – pests!

It was so hard to see the saplings suffer the pest menace. But we had this philosophy that insects were an integral part of the ecosystem and every organism had a place in the larger scheme of things. Besides, I believed that plants needed to face some struggle in order to come up strong and resilient. We couldn't keep protecting them always. When they came up despite the hardships, they would be able to overcome anything that came their way later.

Much like my parenting philosophy – Don't shelter them too much! I tried not to make it easy for my kids, but invariably I felt our kids were growing up in a protective bubble. The world out there was so scary for us parents that we became helpless.

I realised that at least within the safe confines of our homes, we must let them work their way out rather than offering them easy solutions. I always found some parenting lessons hidden in gardening.

It was so heartbreaking to witness pest menace, but though I was afraid this would happen, I had made peace with it. Of course it was bound to happen. We prepared the soil, sowed the seeds, took care of manuring, tackled the weeds and now it was pest problem right on time!

It was difficult to see the pests devouring the carefully grown plants, but when you saw them as a part of the ecosystem where they were there to thrive and live a life and complete a lifecycle too, your perspective changed. You could not have butterflies to pollinate your flowers if you didn't want caterpillars eating your plants! Every organism had a purpose and role in the environment.

I had come to wonder how our idea of gardening itself was so flawed. Gardening and farming had become a transactional relationship between a human and his plants. 'I' sow, 'I' water, and therefore only 'I' shall reap the rewards. Of course, we should, but there were so many more elements to it.

When we garden, we were not just in a relationship with the plant we grow, but with the microbes in the soil, the earthworms, insects (both the beneficial ones and the pests), the sun, the rain, the wind, the soil – all of these biotic and abiotic components had a huge role to play in it. We thought we alone were doing all the work, but in reality, the other elements were at work too, contributing and interacting in their own unique way.

It was a complex amalgamation of interdependency at play than what met the eye. We needed to be aware of this and acknowledge its presence.

Gardening therefore, was not an anthropocentric activity. When I brought my awareness to this aspect, it became a much deeper and more meaningful association. I was trying to bring that cognizance in my farming approach and it had completely shifted my perception about pests as I watched them and tried to learn about them. I had grown to appreciate them and that had completely transformed the way I looked at insects on my farm.

Of course, I used some of the tried and tested organic pest repellents like the neem oil emulsion and the 3G spray from time to time, but I also made sure to grow trap crops as companion planting to manage pests holistically. It had definitely helped to a large extent in managing the pest situation on my farm.

Neem oil emulsion:

1. *Take the juice of one soap nut rind by soaking and squeezing it in 200 ml water for 2-3 hours. (In case of using liquid soap, use 2-3 drops)*
2. *Filter the same and to that add 2.5 ml neem oil. Stir well till all the oil mixes completely.*

3. *Add this to one litre water and shake well.*
4. *Spray on pest affected plants.*

Making 3G spray: 3G solution is also called Agni Asthra.

1. *Take equal measure of green chillies, garlic and ginger.*
2. *Grind the 3 into a fine paste in a mixer along with some water.*
3. *Filter the solution and keep it separately.*
4. *Take one part of this solution and add 10 parts of water and dilute it. (1:10 dilution)*
5. *Spray it on infected plants.*

***

September 2018

Our first snake gourd! How did I miss seeing the fruit formation in its nascent stage? The snake gourd vines covered the whole trellis. Probably it was hidden under all the foliage. Spotting it today took us by surprise. It was almost a foot long and we literally jumped in joy seeing it!

I mean, did we really grow this all by ourselves? It was so special and the feeling was so incredible. I stood frozen near the trellis, watching that snake gourd hanging from the canopy of leaves and beautiful exquisite white flowers. I was awestruck.

I heard Mani call out to me. There was a slight squeal in his voice and I turned to see him beaming ear to ear. He was staring at another trellis and this time it was a cucumber! An unusually large, misshapen cucumber! Nothing like the ones we were used to seeing in the markets. But it was the most beautiful one for us. We stood there watching it and smiling through our sweat-drenched faces, feeling absolutely blissful.

There were many firsts after that and we discovered new vegetables and flowers and beautiful bugs too. Everything was like magic unfolding in front of us. We were like little kids discovering the beauty of nature for the first time. I was falling hopelessly in love with all that I was experiencing. There were lady's finger and tomatoes, pumpkin and beets. Yes, beets too!

The vegetables on my farm made me experiment a lot in my kitchen too. I was making preserves to make sure I used them as long as I could. This was another one of those 'never have I ever thought I'd be doing this' moments, and I had had so many of those in recent times.

I was learning a lot about the seasons of the crops too. There were some that thrived in a particular season, giving me clues about seasonal vegetables. I was recording my findings of what worked best in which season for future references.

I was beginning to realize how important it was to keep a log book. See, it was easy to forget what worked for which plant, what helped and what didn't, how many days after sowing did a particular plant flower or fruit, and so on.

Recording was definitely helping me. Some of the seeds I had planted of cabbage, onion, carrot and lettuce never saw daylight. So predictably they weren't suited for our climate. This did not discourage me. I would anyway try sowing them again in October or November time frame, when it was a bit cooler in Chennai.

The seasons on the farm ebbed and flowed as the seasons came and went, so did the scene on the farm.

> *Live in each season as it passes; breathe the air, drink the drink, taste the fruit, and resign yourself to the influence of the earth.*
>
> —Henry David Thoreau

As we started growing our own vegetables, we noticed something. We were getting some vegetables in abundance during a particular season and then we had none of that for a while. Instead, we had another set of veggies growing abundantly in the other season.

It so happened that we ended up eating more of a particular vegetable during a period of time, and then had to go without it for a certain period and got to eat a few other varieties that grew well in that particular season. Growing our own food taught us to eat along with the seasons!

Somehow, in our modern society, we had reached a point where we got all varieties of vegetables and fruits all year round. But, our farm journey had been teaching us patience and to wait for a crop until it was the right season to grow it. It also nudged us towards learning ways to preserve it and make it last a little bit longer. It taught us that starving for a particular vegetable made it that much sweeter when we finally got to eat it later in the season.

It was an important and most profound lesson we learnt. That we couldn't dictate terms to nature; we needed to surrender to its intelligent ways, because nature knew best!

This was the season of gourds and we had plenty of it. Every week we harvested loads of ridge gourd, bottle gourds and pumpkins. And I knew that in a few weeks, I wouldn't have these. Later in the months, I would be harvesting tomatoes and brinjals. Oh, the loads of delicious tomatoes that would be made into jars of chutneys, pickles, chunky marinara sauce, ketchup and maybe some sun-dried and some frozen for later use.

Then there would be a season when we'd have all kinds of beans – the winged beans, clove beans, broad beans, French beans, long beans, purple beans and many more. And this continued season after season. Yes, it got a bit monotonous, but then we also missed them for a considerable period of time before they reappeared along with the seasons, and that made us long for them again.

This fasting and feasting was how we had started living now. It was honouring the cycle of nature and cycle of life. That was the beauty of food consumption I was introduced to by my farm. It showed me to live with the seasons.

Chapter 27

October 2018

It'd been raining tomatoes on the farm. As we learned to grow crops, we learned something new every time. Like our earlier lesson from growing lady's finger and brinjal taught us that we needed to master succession planting, and do it well, if we needed a continuous supply. We had missed planting the next round of seeds and ended up not having any lady finger or brinjal once the crops came to the end of their lifecycle.

In another lesson, we realised that we must sow a few extra seeds just in case some seeds didn't end up sprouting well. And I guess we ran with that lesson a bit too far with our tomatoes. We thought, we could never plant too many of these, because we'd always need tomatoes. And guess what! Tomatoes, tomatoes everywhere. We were harvesting truckloads!

Well, we were certainly learning. Sometimes we planted too little of something and sometimes too much of something. But I was totally blissed out at the sight of the bright reds, shiny greens and mosaic of green and reds; tomatoes in all different stages of ripening!

The same story goes with our pumpkins too. My vegetable patch was a jungle now with the pumpkin creeper spread all over. I could have a pumpkin hunt organised for kids to come and pick their own pumpkins right in time for Halloween. There were tons of pumpkins and the sight of them filled us up with gratitude.

I was making a mental note to collect a variety of recipes to use up my pumpkins, including pumpkin pie, soup and curries. It was a good thing that this veggie stored well up to four months at room temperature. So I didn't have to worry much about storage.

Our ash gourds were looking mighty fine as well. Especially, the one hanging for dear life from atop the moringa tree. Uff... as if it didn't have any other place to grow. But if it had chosen to hang in there, then who was I to question it?

This took me back to the time when M was just a baby. She was a terrible sleeper who would pull all-nighters every single night, and sleep in small instalments during the day. This meant that I could neither sleep during the night, nor catch a wink during the day. I was a walking-talking zombie for about a year till she started sleeping through the night.

During those times, I learnt the hard way not to try adjusting a sleeping child into a comfortable position. I would wait and wait for her to fall asleep and very gently slide her on to the bed, only to see that she had moved/turned to a certain 'uncomfortable' position. Overcome by my motherly affection, I would try gentle manoeuvres to get her back to a comfortable position, only to end up with a screeching baby.

The point of it is that 'comfortable' and 'uncomfortable' was all from my perspective, not the baby's. I should have let the baby decide what's comfortable for her. Let them be! Parenting lesson from the ash gourd here.

Beans, what can I say? We had all different kinds of them. I harvested the regular French beans, broad beans, string beans and cluster beans, but also some of the rare heirloom varieties that hadn't been in the market for more than thirty years.

The clove beans, winged beans and purple beans were a sight to behold. We stood in the middle of our garden dazed at the bounty. We were like kids in a candy store looking at some exotic candies.

We were learning furiously; gathering all the little nuggets of wisdom our garden threw at us; assimilating all the mistakes we did into lessons learnt.

After months of hard work, sweat and heartbreak, look where it had gotten us! The abundant harvest was unbelievable, to say the least. My farm to table dream had finally come to fruition. We had been harvesting enough produce for our family of four.

From radish, cucumber, cluster beans, tomatoes, bottle gourds, snake gourds, lady finger, brinjal, chillies, beetroot, pumpkin and so many more. We had been able to get more than thirty-five different varieties of vegetables from my farm, all grown absolutely organically without any added fertiliser or pesticide. What a sense of accomplishment! If that didn't make one hopeful of making it as an organic farmer, what would?

As I gathered the abundant load of tomatoes in two baskets, I felt so grateful and blessed. I was already thinking of jars filled with delicious marinara sauce, tomato pickle and maybe some sun-dried tomatoes for later use.

Once we got back home, we sorted all the produce and segregated the ones we needed to refrigerate and the excess produce was placed in a separate pile to invite friends and families to take some home. Once that was sorted, I was all set to whip up a big batch of marinara sauce. I cleared up the dining table to do the prepping and pulled out my recipe notebook. Here's the best marinara sauce recipe you'll ever find. Simple yet oh-so-delicious!

My perfect recipe for marinara sauce (for pizzas and pastas)

Ingredients:

Tomatoes—250 g (finely chopped)
*Onions—*½ cup (finely chopped)
Garlic—3 cloves (finely chopped)
Olive oil—1 tablespoon
*Sugar--*½ tsp
*Salt—*½ tsp (to taste)
Fresh basil (chopped)—1 tablespoon
Fresh parsley—1 tsp
*Oregano (dried)—*½tsp
*Paprika/red chilli flakes—*½tsp
*Pepper powder—*½ teaspoon
(You can use dried basil and parsley too)

Procedure:

Heat one tblsp olive oil in a pan, add garlic and stir.

Add finely chopped onions to it and sauté till translucent. Take time to cook the onions on medium heat to develop some deep flavours.

Add finely chopped tomatoes to it.

Stir in the herbs, spices and salt.

Cook on medium to low heat for about 45 minutes. (Yes, time is the key factor to a great tasting sauce.)

Keep stirring occasionally and cover the pan towards the end as it may start splattering while it thickens.

When the sauce reaches a spreading consistency, remove from heat and cool it.

Blend the mixture in a food processor or mixer for smoother consistency.

If you like it chunky, you can skip the last step.

Marinara/Pizza sauce is now ready.

After distributing excess produce to my neighbours and friends, and preparing jars of marinara sauce and tomato pickle, I was now on to trying my hand at making my own tomato ketchup. The abundant produce had made me experiment a lot in my kitchen. I was working on lots of farm-to-table recipes and cooking had taken centre stage.

As a family we were having lots of delicious farm-fresh food every day. My dream of feeding my family with clean, pesticide free, organic produce had finally come true!

***

During this month, we planned and organised an open house to invite people over to visit our farm. It was wonderful to receive and show the visitors around and share our farm journey with them. People from near and far gathered there and we had a hearty time connecting with them over cups of coffee and our mutual love for gardening.

November 2018

I had quite an interesting observation during my experiments with growing crops. This observation completely changed my perspective on the need to save seeds. I was always under the impression that I really didn't have to go to all the trouble of saving seeds, I could just purchase them from my trusty sources. I mean why should every gardener save seeds? Why, when we could easily procure it. Why waste your time and effort to do that? Well, here's why.

We had planted various seeds during the sowing season (July) and we also sowed ladyfingers. We had grown ladyfinger in bags even before we got our raised garden beds ready. And, therefore, we had some seeds saved from that crop.

But once we started sowing seeds on our raised beds, we

completely forgot about these seeds and used only the ones we had bought during an organic expo.

Though the ladyfinger plant was growing okay, it didn't seem to be coming up at the rate it should be and we never thought much of it at that time. Then a month or so later, we realised we had some seeds saved from our own ladyfinger crop and decided to use them to start another separate batch.

Now, what do you know? These latter ones grew leaps and bounds and started fruiting gloriously while the other previously planted one was just barely producing a few here and there.

So, moral of the story for me was that the seeds I saved from the plants that had grown on my piece of land were definitely much better as the plant has gotten acclimatised to my place, soil and water conditions. They would definitely yield better because they had adapted themselves to the climatic conditions and also developed better pest resistance.

I realised then that seed saving was the most sensible and valuable asset for any gardener. Because now you had the seed of a plant that had already lived on your soil and knew the place better. With more familiarity, wasn't it going to be easy for this guy to survive and adapt better than some foreign seed which was collected from a plant that had grown somewhere else?

With this newly-acquired gyan, I started documenting my process of saving seeds of different variety of vegetables. The more I read on this topic, the more interesting and intriguing it got. There was a way to harvest seeds from different vegetables.

Now, unlike lady finger, which was left to dry on the plant, for cucumbers we used the wet method of seed removal. All the vegetables that were chosen for seed saving purpose had to be left to ripen on the plant/vine itself. That was how we could harvest the most mature seeds for our next season.

For fleshy veggies like tomatoes, cucumber, pumpkin, squash etc:

1. *Remove the seeds and allow them to ferment in a bowl of lukewarm water for three days. This will help in removing the gel coating surrounding the seeds.*
2. *Stir this concoction daily. This fermentation process kills viruses and separates the good seeds from the pulp and the bad seeds.*
3. *The good seeds will sink to the bottom while the bad seeds and pulp will float at the surface.*
4. *Pour the pulp, water and bad seeds carefully using a strainer after the three days.*
5. *Transfer the good seeds on to a paper towel to remove excess moisture.*
6. *Spread them on a plate/paper and air dry them for a few days.*
7. *Store completely dry seeds in a dry air-tight container.*
8. *Use the seeds within 3 to 6 months as they might lose potency.*

For bitter gourd:

Remove seeds from ripened bitter gourds. Wash the pulp off by gently rubbing them in a bowl of water. Remove the pulp and place the seeds in a paper towel. Once dry, place them on a plate and let them air dry for a few days before storing them in an air-tight container.

For brinjal & chillies:

Take the ripened brinjal and chillies and gently make a slit and remove the seeds. Place them on a plate and allow them to air dry to remove any wetness before storing them in an air-tight container.

Vegetable crops were slowly coming to the end of their life cycle, and it was time to save the seeds for the next season. It was also the time to better our skills at succession croppng so we could get a regular supply of the seasonal veggies.

Our weekends completely changed. We now spent the weekends tending to the garden, sowing, weeding, composting and manuring. Evenings went by in recording our learnings from our gardening experience. Our dinner table discussions involved planning and learning ways to build our existing soil structure naturally. As we spent more time on the farm, our understanding of the plant world exploded exponentially.

Currently, our next set of crops were at different stages of growth and we would continue to sow as the weeks passed. As the seasons ended, we went back and did all of this, all over again.

Chapter 28

April 2021

I was sitting in my farmhouse kitchen with my brown diary and a clipboard with a few sheets of one-side used paper. I was desperately trying to draw up a plan for companion planting in a new patch that I was envisioning on my front yard, in the space between some of my tree saplings. But I found myself concentrating instead on the flowering guava tree outside the window and the milky flowers that looked pristine against the green leaves.

I once again brought my attention back to my chart and found myself wondering about the ginger I sowed in the corner patch. A moment later, flower garden beckoned too. With my mind wandering, I realised this wasn't the time to work. This was the time to just be; to revel in the reality of what was once just a dream.

Work could wait.

I got up and moved out to my front porch and sat on the steps. I wanted to smell, taste, and savour the fruits of my labour. I wanted to feel the breeze that brought the scent of the plants I grew from seeds on a barren land. I wanted to hear the bird calls that seemed to come from my Singapore cherry tree that I had planted just to invite these beautiful creatures into my garden.

I saw my white painted pergola filled with bright pink bougainvillea and yellow alamanda. My eyes feasted on all that was on my farm. Even as I was seeing all of them, a part of me felt like I was missing them already. My eyes couldn't seem to have enough of it. I desperately wanted to experience more of all this. The pleasure of seeing my dream, also brought a certain ache within.

I suddenly felt such sadness for those who don't get to access a garden; to take a stroll along the crooked paths, hear the symphony of birdsongs, and see butterflies flitting about on the blue porter weeds, wedelia and lantana. It was a delight I wouldn't want anyone to miss in their lifetime. To witness the painfully beautiful teeny-tiny details of a garden was a luxury I didn't take lightly.

I felt like the richest person when I was in my garden. It was usually the not-so-obvious details of my garden that reduced me to tears; that these weeds with their exquisite flowers, the bugs with their jewel like shimmer wouldn't ever grace the covers of any gardening magazine, made me weep. I didn't think my two eyes were enough to drink in this beauty. I just couldn't get enough.

I felt desperate and helpless and on some days even frustrated to not have the capacity to feel all of this beyond my five senses. I felt deeply pained by this inadequacy and within an instance, found myself brimming with inexplicable joy! I don't know how I could feel these contradictory emotions all at once, but I often found myself in this quandary.

Could I experience all of this in a more immersive way? In an attempt to see if I could relish it more, I closed my eyes. I wanted to see if my other senses would take this experience to a greater level.

I wanted to inhale the scents of my farm deeply; I wanted to feel the sunlight trickling in through the palm fronds land gently on my eyelids; I wanted the cool breeze to tickle my sweaty cheeks; I wanted to hear the many different sounds of birds and critters, some chirping nearby from neem trees and some cooing from a far-off place.

There were also a few rooster crows coming in from a neighbour's farm. I sat there for I don't know how long. With my eyes closed, I could feel that the sun was slowly setting in the horizon. The intensity of the sunlight was milder and the breeze cooler.

I felt the urge to brew some tea and move to the 'four tree point' that was in front of the house, so I could envelop myself in the warm embrace of my farm before it drowned in the darkness of the night.

Here, we were learning to live with the seasons. Seasons on the farm continued to teach us incredibly valuable lessons as we learnt to nurture the soil. In times of unprecedented technology and ease, as a society, we had done away with everything that grounded us and provided us with a sense of connection.

Farming gave us that purpose. It was teaching us the value of deeper connection with nature. It had provided us with not only an abundance of fresh food, but vitality of mind, body and spirit in the short amount of time we got to experience it. It nurtured our senses with its bounty, something that had been missing from our lives for so long!

I have to say that I had discovered the pleasure of physical work, learned that good food is at the centre of a good life and had fallen hopelessly in love with this farm life.

The awakening of a wider ecological consciousness requires the acknowledgment and celebration of our reciprocal relationship with the rest of the living world. For only when we can hear the languages of other beings are we capable of understanding the generosity of the earth, and learning to give our own gifts in return.

> *Knowing that you love the earth changes you, activates you to defend and protect and celebrate. But when you feel that the earth loves you in return, that feeling transforms the relationship from a one-way street into a sacred bond.*
>
> — Braiding Sweetgrass

I looked back on the initial days of building my farm and reflected upon the impatient days, months and years it took to reach where I was; to live the life that I dreamed of; of growing my own vegetables from seed; of living a farm to table lifestyle. And, the many hours of toiling in the sun and rain, caring for my plants and the many hours of planning, processing and yearning that went into finally realising this dream.

The burst of freshness and goodness wasn't all that I got in living a life of a farmer! With every bite, I got that elusive deep sense of satisfaction – the invisible secret ingredients, the blood, sweat and tears that combined in those moments to create a deep appreciation for all that went into the life that fed us and nourished us. There was magic in this food. Food that was medicine to not just our body, but our soul too.

As we looked ahead to another busy season on the farm, it was so important that I reflected upon this magic. It had to be magic; there was no other way to explain this. Because every single morsel of food that was grown on this farm came from severe effort (yes, let there be no doubt in that!), and from hearts filled with love for what we got to do and a certain joy that was infectious.

Why did this form of food matter? Why toil when food was available so cheaply for much lesser effort? Because convenience food didn't do much except fill the space in our bellies; there was nothing nourishing or meaningful about it.

There was nothing satisfying about grabbing a go-to fast food and gulping it down while driving or running errands. Instead, think what a meal could do if you had a hand in growing at least some part of it; even just a handful of homegrown herb to garnish. Wouldn't that feed your soul much more?

I was in no way against convenience stores. I was simply encouraging myself to make my food experience richer and as meaningful as it could get. As I explored, I found that the richness of a meaningful existence came only when we put our hands in the soil and laboured to grow the food that we served our families.

That sense of purpose which I was missing in today's modern life was found in these moments of creating things with my hands. Living life in close proximity to nature, satisfied that special craving within me. This life, this farm life, this had my heart! This was so beautiful, so difficult, so exhilarating, so taxing yet so out-of-the-world joyful. This was as good as it could get, and I absolutely believed that.

I deeply felt that in our own ways, we all need to be earth keepers; we need to nurture, build and steward. We need to be guardians of the precious resources nature provided for all of us. We couldn't be just takers.

We needed to pause our advancements, if all it did was deplete and destroy the very source of life. There was a much richer and deeper way to experience this one life than what our shallow culture gave us. I wished that everyone got to experience this!

Afterword

It was the peak of summer and the garden was bursting with colours. There was a deep sense of gratitude that filled my heart. To be able to create this heaven from scratch couldn't have been possible without divine intervention!

It would soon be time to harvest toor dal from the six trees we planted a couple of years back. The chillies had ripened enough to be harvested and taken for drying and processing chilli powder. There was manuring to be done for all the fruit trees. There were coconuts drying in the driveway that needed to be de-shelled and taken to the oil mill for coconut oil processing.

We had an abundance of turmeric harvest and I had packed few pouches of turmeric powder for my farm helpers that needed to be handed out. And there were loads of miscellaneous tasks waiting for us.

But we were there. We were there planting patches of yams and building trellises for the gourds. We were there working and training the bougainvillea up the pergola. We were there with sore backs and content hearts. We were there for it all.

Acknowledgements

This book has been in the making for many years now. Writing this book has been a cathartic experience as it allowed me to relive and relish every bit of the journey I undertook in realising my farm dream. I have so many people to be thankful for in this transformative journey.

First and foremost, I want to thank my husband for his rock-solid support and for trusting my vision. The dream would've remained a mere dream without you.

To my kids, for being a constant source of joy and for being the biggest teachers in my life. I learn so much from you every day. Immense gratitude and love to my family and friends.

My heartfelt thanks to my incredible literary agent, Suhail Mathur of The Book Bakers literary agency for his faith in my book and for the constant support and guidance. He has been instrumental in bringing this book into the world.

To my amazing publisher, Mr. Arup Bose of Srishti Publishers, thank you for believing in my book and for extending a warm welcome into the Srishti family.

I am immensely grateful to my wonderful editor, Stuti Gupta, for her invaluable inputs, guidance and insights throughout the process. I am incredibly touched by the warmth, support and kindness extended by team Srishti, every step of the way. It's been an honour and privilege to work alongside an amazing team like yours.

I am extremely grateful for the valuable contributions of Alladi Mahadevan, who has been a mentor and guide in my organic farming journey.

I want to extend my thanks to Dr Sultan Ahmed Ismail for his teachings and wisdom.

My gratitude to Raghukumar and his amazing OGF group for providing a steadfast support system.

To the legendary Solar Suresh, thank you for your generosity of spirit and guidance.

To Parameshwaran of Aadiyagai, thank you for the work you do, and Kiruba Shankar for your inspiration.

To my dear friend Shivani Salil, I have no words to describe the unrelenting support and kindness you have shown me. You have been there since the book was in its first draft. Your words of encouragement had been monumental in making me believe in my book. You have not just been my very first beta reader and editor, but also a friend, philosopher and guide. Thank you for everything.

My special thanks to Penmancy. Winning their pitchfest opened doors for my book in amazing ways.

Special thanks to my dear friend Meha Sharma and all my writing community friends for being my cheerleaders and my inspiration.

Last but not the least, I am extremely grateful for my beautiful blog readers, and my wonderful online community. Without your engagement, interest and curiosity in my farming journey, this book would not have materialised. Thank you.